# EGO XPOSED

by

Rekeita Bradford-Jones

ISBN: 978-1-7344033-7-4

Editing: Y B XPOSED Publishing

Cover Design: Finesse Logos by Kiki

Printed in the United States of America.

i

# DEDICATION

To every woman who ever had to lead when she wanted to be led.

To every man brave enough to look in the mirror without flinching.

This book is for the builders, the believers, and the broken.

The ones who never stopped showing up, even when they were sick of starting over.

To the power couples who don't look like the fairytales and work for each other daily.

To the ones still learning how to love in truth, not ego. And to the one man who saw all of me and still chose me.

Wack 100.

You didn't just change my life.

You gave me room to finally live it.


This book is ours.


— R Ann B

# HOW TO READ THIS BOOK

## Understanding the Flow of EGO XPOSED

This isn't just a relationship book.

It's a layered unfolding of two people; raw, healed, unfinished, and honest.

The structure of **EGO XPOSED** follows the rhythm of how love works:

First, with self.

Then, through connection.

And finally, together as one.

Here's how the book is broken down:

## CHAPTERS 1–4

### Written by R ANN B

These chapters take you inside her personal evolution, emotional strength, survival, faith, heartbreak, and healing it took to become a woman who could love without losing herself. Before she ever loved him, she faced herself.

## CHAPTERS 5–8

**Written by WACK 100**

Now it's his turn. These chapters are Wack's voice; raw, unfiltered, and real. He opens up about the emotional habits he had to break, the vulnerability it took to be present, and what it means for a man to show up for a woman like her truly.

## CHAPTERS 9–20

**Written by Both**

This is where they meet, page for page, ego to ego, love to love. Every chapter alternates between their perspectives, showing how two powerful individuals learned to lead, heal, and build together. It's not a fairytale. It's legacy.

## BONUS CHAPTER

To close the book, you'll find a special bonus chapter. One last moment of truth, insight, and transparency—designed to leave you full, not just inspired.

Read it with your heart open.

Read it like a mirror.

Read it like the healing you didn't know you needed.

# TABLE OF CONTENTS

# INTRODUCTION

## EGO XPOSED

## WHY WE HAD TO TELL IT ALL

**R ANN B**

They say love is blind, but ego will snatch the blindfold off real quick. This movement didn't start from peace. It started from pressure. From arguing in closed rooms and pretending in public. From me wanting to talk, and him wanting silence. From truth so loud, even the lies got uncomfortable.

We were tired of hearing relationship experts who never lived what we lived. Tired of the fake goals of couples showing you flowers but not the funeral behind them.

So, we said: Let's talk for real. Let's expose the ego. His. Mine. Yours. Everybody's.

**WACK 100**

Look, I'm not going to sugarcoat it. Most dudes out here are ego-driven. Hell, we were raised that way.

1

Don't talk about your feelings. Don't look weak. Don't let her run you.

But at some point, all that pride, that shit starts costing you peace.

R Ann B and I have been through it. We still go through it. But what makes us different is that we're not afraid to put it on the table. The wins, the Ls, the ugly arguments at 3 a.m.

Our Podcast wasn't about being perfect. It was about being honest. This book? Even more so.

This Chapter Is About:

- How ego shows up before love even gets a chance to breathe.
- Why we chose to expose our flaws instead of hiding them.
- The difference between protecting the relationship and protecting your image.
- Why silence is often the biggest betrayal in relationships.

- What we learned from starting the podcast and what we're still learning.

## R ANN B

I had to get to a place where my voice mattered more than my fear. Fear of being judged. Fear of being labeled too emotional, too strong, too much.

But women like me, we hold a lot. We heal, we hustle, we help everybody else… but who helps us?

When I stopped trying to be quiet to keep him comfortable, we actually started growing. Not instantly. Not easily. But honestly.

## WACK 100

A lotta times, men don't even realize how much we weaponize silence. We think we're being calm or protecting peace, when really, we're shutting shit down before it can even breathe.

This podcast forced me to listen. To speak. To admit when I was tripping. And trust me, admitting that in front of thousands of people, that's different. But it's also powerful.

**BEHIND THE MIC**

We argue, laugh, make up and challenge each other. But most of all, we don't lie to y'all. That's what EGO XPOSED is about.

**R ANN B**

There's this moment nobody talks about. It's not when you fall in love. It's not even when things fall apart. It's that in-between space when you're both sitting in silence, realizing that love alone won't fix what ego broke.

I remember laying in bed next to him, both of us wide awake, backs turned, no words. That wasn't distance. That was pride. That was both of us knowing we had something worth saving... but waiting on the other person to say it first.

**WACK 100**

And that right there, that's where a lot of relationships die. Not from cheating or yelling, but from ego. From two people knowing they want to fight for it, but being too stubborn to throw the first punch of peace.

You gotta ask yourself, what's more important, being right, or being real? I used to think apologizing meant I was weak. Now I know holding it in just meant I didn't trust that it would be received. That would have killed my ego.

## R ANN B

We made this podcast and now this book because we needed a space to be unapologetically ourselves. No filters, no PR team, no damage control. Just two people in love, working through it, unafraid to get messy. And if we can expose our egos to grow together, maybe you can too.

## WACK 100

Let's be clear, this ain't therapy. We're not here to preach. We're not licensed to heal anybody. But we lived this, and we're still living it.

Have you ever been in a relationship where you felt like your voice was loud, but still not heard? That's where ego thrives. I had to learn that just because I provide, it doesn't mean I'm present. Just because I'm protecting her doesn't mean I'm connected to her. Ego will trick a man into thinking silence is strength. But sometimes, silence is sabotage.

**R ANN B**

And women, we've got our own ego, too. Mine looked like hyper-independence. Like, "I got it," when really I wanted help. Like shutting down emotionally but still expecting him to read my mind.

I had to stop weaponizing my emotions the same way he had to stop hiding his. This wasn't just about healing us. It was about unlearning patterns we were both raised with.

You can't build a future when you're dragging broken blueprints from the past. Trust me, I'm a subject matter expert in the building field.

**WACK 100**

Sometimes she'd be talking, and I'd be nodding, but I wasn't really there. That's ego, too. Just being in the room doesn't mean you're a part of the relationship.

When I started listening, not to respond but to understand, things started to change. She'd soften up, and things became a lot smoother, which meant less stress and more clarity. Shit sign me up for that any day.

## R ANN B

This chapter isn't just the intro to our book. It's a mirror. If you're reading this, ask yourself:

- Where is ego running your relationship?
- What conversations are you avoiding?
- What apologies are you too proud to say?

Because that's where your healing begins.

## WACK 100

At the end of the day, ego ain't the enemy. It's how you use it. Ego can either be armor—or a cage. I had to learn how to drop mine just enough to let her in… and trust me, that's harder than it sounds. Because real intimacy?

It ain't just about sex or dates or gifts. It's about letting somebody see the parts of you that ain't polished. The parts you're still working on.

That's what we're doing here. That's what this book is about.

**R ANN B**

The world sees the power couple. They see the wins, the hustle, the chemistry. But they don't see the work. The breakdowns. The days we didn't like each other but still chose to show up.

This is us taking off the masks.

If you made it this far, you're not just a reader, you're part of the conversation now. So, sit with what made you uncomfortable. Rewind what hit too close. Because if ego builds walls… truth tears them down.

**TOGETHER**

This book isn't here to fix you. It's here to reveal you. If we had to unlearn the habits, the pride, the silence, the shutdowns, so do you. The goal isn't to be ego-free. It's to be ego-aware.

And in that awareness, you give love a real chance to thrive. This isn't just our story, it's a shared awakening. We wrote this to expose the part of love that most people tend to hide. The pride, the pain, the power struggles, and the growth.

If you've ever lain next to someone you love and still felt miles away. If you've ever stayed silent when you should've spoken or fought to be heard, but didn't know how to say it right.

This chapter was written for you. We're not perfect. We're present. We're not healed. We're healing. But most of all, we're committed to staying in the room when ego tries to run, because the only way to grow real love… is to stay honest in the mirror. Let's build!

# CHAPTER 1
# THE MASK WAS MINE

# CHAPTER 1

## THE MASK WAS MINE

Before I ever let anyone close, I made sure I faced myself first. I didn't point fingers. Not at the man. Not at the pain. Not even at the people who should've shown up and didn't. Because truth is—I've always taken accountability. Even when I wasn't the villain. Even when silence would've been easier.

I knew early on: nobody was coming to rescue me. So, I learned to rescue myself and with that came the mask. It didn't come with glitter or arrogance. It came with responsibility. It came with strength people admired but never questioned. It came with being the one who "got it all together", even when I didn't. I didn't just wear the mask. I became it. Because when you grow up being the fixer, the nurturer, the rock. You stop expecting to be handled with care.

That's what ego becomes for women like me, a shield, not for dominance but for survival. I smiled when I was overwhelmed. I loved when I was empty. I served while silently starving. Not because I was pretending. But because I didn't believe I had permission to fall apart.

Vulnerability didn't scare me; disappointment did. I didn't fear being seen. I feared being seen and still left. So, I made sure I was needed. Necessary. Valuable. Indispensable. But underneath the applause and the roles, I was still that girl—wanting to be chosen, not for what I give, but for who I am when I'm not performing.

I wasn't hiding behind ego because I thought I was better. I was hiding behind strength because I was afraid of being too much, too honest, too emotional. Too soft. Masks don't just block pain. They block love. They block rest. They block the very thing you say you want. And healing required me to do something terrifying: Put it down. All of it. The armor. The over-functioning. The fear of letting go. Because real love can't meet the version of you that's performing, it can only meet the version of you that's present.

So I stood in the mirror. No makeup. No filters. No titles. Just me. I looked her in the eyes and didn't flinch. Didn't shrink. Didn't criticize. I chose her. Not because she was perfect. But because for the first time... she was real. And that's who he met. Not the mask. Not the version of me who had it all figured out. He met the woman who had finally put her ego down long enough to receive. If I had met him before the mirror, I would've mishandled him. I would've questioned his intentions, tested his consistency, and tried to out prove my own value. Not because I didn't believe in love. But because I hadn't yet believed I deserved it, soft. But when he came... I was ready. Not for a fantasy. Not for a fairytale. But for the kind of reality that doesn't flinch at truth. He didn't need a mask. He needed me present. Grounded. Honest. Healed enough to know I still had healing to do. And I was not perfect, but present. Not desperate, but open. Not guarded but guided.

I did the work before the love arrived. And when it came, I didn't miss it. I didn't sabotage it. I didn't shrink in it. I grew with it. Because the mask taught me how to survive, but the mirror taught me how to love.

## R ANN B – EGO XPOSED TAKEAWAY:

- I didn't blame others for my pain; I faced it head-on, even when it was heavy.

- Ego isn't always loud; sometimes it hides behind high-functioning, perfection, and silence.

- The mask I wore wasn't to impress; it was to survive.

- Healing didn't require someone else's apology. It required my honesty.

- Love didn't find me when I was performing. It found me when I was present.

- The mirror didn't break me; it introduced me to the woman I was always becoming.

# CHAPTER 2

# PROVIDER VS PROTECTER

# CHAPTER 2

## PROVIDER vs PROTECTOR

I've always known how to provide for myself. What I didn't know was how it felt to finally be protected.

There's a difference between a man who pays for you… and a man who covers you. And I say that as someone who didn't just provide for herself but for her sons, too. I wasn't out here chasing men. I wasn't rotating dates or looking to be chosen. I was focused on building, on healing, on surviving. I was the backbone of my household, the leader of my life, and the sole provider for my family.

There were seasons I was so locked in that love wasn't even a thought. Not because I didn't want it, but because I didn't have the luxury of prioritizing it. My life required discipline, strategy, and sacrifice. And I wore those responsibilities like armor. Not because I wanted to be hard, but because I couldn't afford to be soft. I made peace with carrying it alone. Because I didn't see another option. I didn't wait on a man to save me; I saved myself.

So no, I didn't know what protection felt like. Not in the way I gave it to others. Not in the way I needed it for myself. I was so used to being the safe space that I forgot I was worthy of being protected, too. I had only ever experienced men who admired my strength but didn't know how to pour back into it. Who assumed because I was "handling it," I didn't need holding.

When you're the one who everyone leans on, you start to believe your softness is a liability. And that's why Wack changed everything.

He didn't meet a damsel. He met a woman who was holding it all together. And instead of trying to take over, he stood beside me. He made space to rest and brought protection I didn't have to earn. He didn't make me choose between being powerful and being loved. He allowed me to be both. For the first time, I didn't have to trade in my strength to feel safe. Or did I?

Before Wack, I had only experienced people who gave provision through obligation or ego. They gave enough to say they were doing something, but never enough to say they saw me. They didn't know how to protect what they didn't understand. And truthfully, I didn't know how to ask for it. Because how do you request something you've never experienced?

I had made my own table. I was used to pouring into others, covering others, and healing others. But being covered? Being held emotionally, mentally, spiritually? That felt foreign. He didn't just show up with provisions; he showed up with presence. He didn't ask me to stop being strong. He just made sure I didn't have to be strong alone.

I had never been with a man who made me feel that secure. Not just in words, but in action. In consistency. In how he paid attention to what I didn't say. In how he watched over my peace like it was his responsibility, too.

Wack was the first man I didn't have to shrink for or lead. I didn't have to compete for space or perform for love. He didn't make me earn softness; he offered it. And that changed everything.

Before him, I didn't even know how tired I was. How heavy it was to always be the one making sure everything was okay. I had trained myself to live in survival mode, but he gave me permission to rest. He didn't just protect my body; he protected my being. He covered me without controlling me. He led without silencing me. He made it safe to be held, not just touched. I was never afraid to stand on my own. But for the first time in my life, I didn't have to, and that's the difference. A provider will show you what he can give. But a protector will show you what he can carry with you.

## R ANN B – EGO XPOSED TAKEAWAY:

- I wasn't out chasing love. I was building a life, raising sons, and carrying the weight alone.
- I didn't grow up expecting protection, so I became my own provider.
- Being provided for is not the same as being covered.

- Real protection isn't loud, it's consistent, quiet, and safe.

- Wack was the first man who didn't just admire my strength, he protected it.

- I didn't have to give up my power to feel peace.

- A protector doesn't ask you to shrink. He stands beside you while you expand.

# CHAPTER 3
# I DON'T NEED YOU, BUT I WANT YOU

# CHAPTER 3

# I DON'T NEED YOU—BUT I WANT YOU

I built a life without needing a man. But wanting one? That took more strength than I expected.

For a long time, I told myself: "I don't need anyone." And I wasn't lying. I really didn't. I paid the bills. Raised the kids. Built the brand. Led the rooms. Pulled myself out of every dark season I was thrown into, alone.

I was the storm and the shelter. The answer and the backup plan. I was the one who showed up when nobody else did.

So when people said, "You're too strong," what they meant was "You're not desperate."

However, there's a cost to always standing tall. You forget what it feels like to lean.

It took me years to realize that "I don't need you" wasn't strength. It was defense. It was survival. It was protection from being let down.

Because if I didn't need love, love couldn't disappoint me. If I didn't need a partnership, I didn't have to face the ache of not having it.

But there's something even more powerful than being needed: Being wanted. Want is a choice. It's intentional. It says, "I'm not with you because I have to be. I'm here because I see you, I value you, I choose you." And that's what changed everything for me.

There was a time I chose "safe." Not because it fed my soul, but because I believed what I was taught: "God will give you what you need, not what you want."

So, I married a man I didn't love. I made a covenant with compatibility, not chemistry. With logic, not alignment and I called it obedience. I called it spiritual maturity. But deep down, I knew I was settling, not just in partnership, but in desire.

I was so used to choosing what made sense that I stopped believing I was allowed to have what made me feel, and that decision cost me something. When you deny your desires long enough, you start to confuse numbness with peace. I wasn't in love. I was surviving... again. Just this time, with a ring.

When I finally left, I promised myself: Never again would I choose what looked good over what felt right. Never again would I shrink my desires in the name of being "wise." I stopped asking God for what I needed. I started positioning myself for what's designed for me. And when I did... Wack came.

I didn't come to him empty. I came full. Not needy, but ready. Not looking to be saved, just finally open to being seen.

I didn't need a man to complete me. I wanted someone I could glean from. I could love him from the overflow. He didn't validate me; he added value. He didn't fix my life; he respected the one I had already built, and that made all the difference.

There's power in not needing a man. But there's even more power in choosing one, freely, fully, without fear. When love isn't based on survival, it becomes sacred.

When you finally allow yourself to want someone without losing yourself, you realize you're not weaker, you're wiser.

But when you've carried yourself for so long, when you've been your own answer, your own rescue, your own everything, it's hard to trust. It's hard to trust a man who doesn't ask you to prove your worth. One who doesn't compete with your strength but complements it. One who doesn't show up to fix you because he sees you're not broken.

Being wanted is beautiful. But when you've lived in survival, it's terrifying too. There were moments I flinched at softness. Moments, I braced for betrayal because I was so used to being the one left holding it all. There were times I questioned if I was even safe to be loved this deeply without having to earn it.

But this time, I didn't run. I stayed. I leaned in. And slowly… I let myself receive what I had always deserved. Because "I don't need you" used to be my power. But now? "I want you, and I trust you with me"? That's my healing.

## R ANN B – EGO XPOSED TAKEAWAY:

- I didn't come to Wack needing to be saved, I came full.

- "I don't need you" was never about pride. It was survival.

- I once married what felt "safe," not what I truly desired, and I paid the emotional cost.

- Suppressing desire doesn't make you wise. It makes you numb.

- God didn't give me the desire to punish me. He gave it to guide me.

- Real love isn't forced. It flows. It chooses you freely, fully, without performance.

- Wanting someone from wholeness is stronger than needing them from emptiness.

- The greatest flex is letting yourself be loved, not because you need it, but because you know you deserve it.

# CHAPTER 4

# I WAS THE SAFE SPACE
# BUT WHO WAS MINE?

# CHAPTER 4

# I WAS THE SAFE SPACE—BUT WHO WAS MINE?

Everybody leaned on me. But when I needed someone to lean on, the room was empty.

I was the one people called when their world fell apart.

The strong friend.

The go-to.

The fixer.

The anchor.

And I wore that role like a badge. Not because I asked for it. But because I had to. There wasn't time to fall apart. There wasn't space to not know. There wasn't permission to be fragile.

I was too busy catching everyone else. But in the quiet moments. When the doors were closed, when the house was finally still, when nobody needed saving, I broke alone. It's a strange kind of loneliness. Being surrounded but not supported. Being praised but never poured into. Being everyone's peace, while silently craving your own. I was the safe space.

But where was mine? I was the healer. But who held me when I bled? I was the strong one. But strength without softness is just silent suffering.

The truth is… Nobody ever asked if I was okay. They just assumed I'd figure it out, and I usually did. But just because I can carry it doesn't mean I should have to. I had trained people to believe I didn't need help because I didn't know how to receive it. Not without guilt. Not without fear. Not without feeling like a burden.

So I swallowed the breakdowns. I spiritualized the burnout. I called the exhaustion "purpose." I smiled through pain that should've never been mine to carry.

It wasn't just the men who failed to cover me.

It was the world that expected me to cover everyone else. Being in the safe space made me invisible. Because people don't check on the strong ones, they just show up when they need you and disappear when you need them.

But I kept showing up, I kept giving, I kept pouring. Because love, to me, meant being useful. Until one day I realized, I was loving everyone but myself.

I didn't need someone to fix me. I needed someone who wouldn't fold when I got quiet. Someone who didn't panic when I pulled back to breathe. Someone who didn't guilt me for not always being "on." I didn't need advice.

I needed peace. A place to land. A presence that didn't rush me to be better before I was ready. And that's who Wack became for me.

He didn't show up, trying to rearrange me. He didn't try to compete with the woman I had become. He saw my strength, but he also saw my fatigue.

He heard the power in my voice, but he paid attention to the weight in my silence. He didn't love the version of me that everyone else clapped for. He loved the version that was still learning to rest. The version that said, "I'm tired," and didn't feel like she had to apologize for it. With him, I didn't have to be "the strong one" every second. I could be soft. messy. Uncertain and still safe.

That was new for me because I had always associated love with performance.

If I wasn't fixing, pouring, helping, or healing, what value did I bring? But with him, my value wasn't in what I did. It was in who I was.

Even in stillness. Even in silence.

Even when I had nothing to give but my presence. He made it clear I didn't have to earn rest. I didn't have to explain my softness. I didn't have to ask twice to be held. And that...

That was healing. There's a difference between performing out of obligation and serving from a place of peace.

I had spent so much of my life giving because I had to. If I didn't, things would fall apart. Nobody else knew how to show up the way I did. But with him, it was different.

I wasn't giving out of survival. I was giving out of desire. He didn't demand my submission.

He created a space so safe that surrender didn't feel like a sacrifice; it felt like home. I wasn't desperate to prove my worth. I was eager to pour into him. To affirm him. To stand beside him. To honor the man who, for the first time in my life, made me feel covered.

I laid my gifts at his feet, not because I was weak, but because I was finally in the presence of someone who didn't misuse what I carried.

And for a season... I lost myself in him. Not in a toxic way. Not in the way I had feared love would consume me. But in the way a woman does when she's finally safe enough to let her whole self be seen.

I wasn't afraid to lose control. I wasn't guarding my emotions. I let go fully, willingly and softly. And for the first time, I experienced the kind of intimacy that didn't shrink me; it revealed me.

I became one with him. Not just emotionally. But spiritually. Energetically. Intimately. And as beautiful as it was, it frightened me. When you've been your own everything for so long, becoming one with someone else feels like losing yourself. Even if it's exactly what you prayed for.

I found myself wanting to pull back, not because he was unsafe, but because I didn't know who I was without the weight.

I started fighting to reclaim an identity that had served me well in the past... but no longer fit the woman I had become. I wasn't actually losing myself. I was outgrowing her. What I didn't understand at first was that I wasn't being erased. I was being expanded.

The version of me that fought, led, protected, and endured. She brought me here.

But she wasn't built to carry me forward to my next stage.

It wouldn't be rooted in survival. It would be rooted in softness.

This stage, this version of me, was the one I always dreamed of. The one I prayed for but didn't think I could trust. The one I envisioned but didn't believe I'd be allowed to become. The one who could finally rest in love and not lose herself in it.

## R ANN B – EGO XPOSED TAKEAWAY:

- I was everyone's safe space, but for years, I didn't have one of my own.

- Being strong became my identity, but it also became my prison.

- I didn't perform for Wack out of obligation. I poured into him because I was finally safe enough to serve from rest, not survival.

- I laid my gifts at his feet, not to lose myself, but because I trusted he wouldn't misuse them.

- Becoming one with him frightened me not because I was broken, but because I didn't recognize the healed version of myself.

- I thought I was fighting to protect my identity... but I was really fighting to stay in a stage I had already outgrown.

- My next season wasn't a loss of self; it was the becoming of the woman I had always dreamed I'd be.

- Rest isn't weakness, and softness doesn't surrender, and love, when it's real, doesn't erase you, it reveals you.

# CHAPTER 5
# SHE TAUGHT ME HOW TO STAY

# CHAPTER 5
# SHE TAUGHT ME HOW TO STAY

I had always stayed; what I hadn't learned was how to stay mentally present. I didn't run when things got hard; I stayed for decades.

From 14 to 44, I was with the same woman. We had history and family. A bond that was built young before I even knew who I was.

She started as my sweetheart. Over time, I became more than her man—I became her guide. I raised her in a lot of ways. But emotionally? I stayed stuck in the version of myself I had to be for her. And the truth is… I didn't physically leave until a year before I met R Ann B But emotionally? I had checked out long before that.

Staying wasn't about presence. It was about the pattern. I knew how to be loyal. How to provide. How to protect. But I didn't know how to evolve in love.

Then I met a woman who wasn't waiting to be built. She was the builder. She didn't come to me needing answers. She came with a foundation already laid. She didn't need a man to shape her. She needed a man who could meet her—mentally, emotionally, energetically.

R Ann B wasn't a project. She was a mirror. She forced me to ask: Had I ever really stayed out of wholeness, or had I just stayed out of habit?

I heard her before I saw her. We met on an app called Clubhouse. She wasn't performing.

She wasn't pressed. She was just her—articulate, grounded, raw, and real.

Something in me locked in on her instantly.

I pursued her for 9 months before I even got to meet her. Not because she played games—but because she wasn't moved by status or pressure.

She made me wait. She made me grow. She made me lead differently. When we finally met, I was already drawn in. But being around her took it even deeper.

R Ann B served me and waited on me hand and foot. Not because I demanded it—but because it was in her heart to do it. Her alpha was always beta when it came to me. And that humbled me. Because I had never experienced a woman like her—a southern woman with a heart that desired to serve, and all she wanted in return was a safe place to rest.

It wasn't submission out of fear. It was love out of choice. It was respect without compromise. Shit, it felt almost too good to be true.

But it was real, but I knew if I ever wanted to keep it, I'd have to become a man who didn't just stay—but stayed present.

What's wild is that much like me, she had her own frustrations with the religious world, too. She didn't talk about it much, but I could tell it left a mark, not on her belief, but on how people misused it.

She never lost her foundation—but I saw her almost walk away from the part of her that used to shine in that space. And I wasn't about to let that happen. I'd tell her, "Don't throw it all away. That's what made you solid. That's where your strength came from."

Because even if I wasn't all the way tapped in spiritually, I could still recognize truth when I saw it.

She had something real in her. A connection most people couldn't touch. She moved with clarity. She spoke with power. And I knew that light she carried came from somewhere deep.

My father was a preacher. So yeah, I come from it. I just didn't always embrace it.

But even with all the reasons I had to turn away, she sparked something back in me. Not through preaching—but through how she walked.

She started telling me I had a calling, too.

She said, "Wack, you move like a pastor. You lead people, you guide them, you give more than you ever say out loud."

And deep down, I knew she was right. I never needed a mic or a collar. I led in my own way. I covered people who couldn't cover themselves. I moved with purpose, even when the world tried to paint me as reckless.

She didn't try to "fix" my image. She poured into the parts of me nobody applauded.

She saw the giver, the builder and the leader who didn't need a title to make an impact. That made me want to protect her light.

Behind all the noise and judgment, we both came into this with battle scars from faith spaces—but we found peace in each other's presence.

**WACK 100 – EGO XPOSED TAKEAWAY:**

- I didn't run from relationships—I stayed for 30 years. But staying out of obligation isn't the same as staying out of growth.

- I was loyal, present, and committed, but I wasn't emotionally available.

- R Ann B didn't just ask for my time. She asked for my truth.

- She served me without losing herself. Her alpha bowed to mine, and it didn't make either of us smaller; it made us stronger.

- I pursued her for 9 months before we ever met. What I got in return was peace, balance, and a woman who knew how to stand beside me, not behind me.

- I used to have a distaste for anything religious because I felt overlooked by someone who served the church but forgot the home.

- R Ann B didn't push religion. She knew her first ministry was her household, and I felt that.

- She reminded me of the leadership already in me. The part that didn't need a title to guide people or change lives.

- She didn't try to fix my image. She enhanced my light.

- She didn't teach me how to stay; she showed me why it was finally safe to.

# CHAPTER 6

# MAKE LOVE TO HER SPIRIT

# CHAPTER 6

# MAKE LOVE TO HER SPIRIT

"You been in bodies. But you've never been in presence." I'd had sex, plenty of sex. I knew what to do physically. How to take control. Mentally as well. But I was connected to her mind, body, and spirit?

To me, sex had always been a release, a power move, a rhythm I could control. A way to silence everything else. But nobody ever taught me how to slow down and feel it. To stay in it, not just the act, but the energy. Nobody ever taught me how to make love with my mind and not just my body. Until her!

R Ann B wasn't impressed by performance. She could feel when my body was present, but my spirit wasn't. She did not need me to break her back—she needed me to break down the walls between us.

And that was new to me. I had never been with a woman who called me deeper in the middle of it. Not louder but deeper.

She could stop me mid-stroke and say, "You left me. Come back." She wasn't talking about my position. She was talking about my presence.

This woman taught me how to move with intention. She made me look her in the eyes—not just when I wanted her, but when I needed her, when I was vulnerable. When I didn't have it all together, she forced me to open up and talk about the weight I had to carry.

She taught me that real intimacy wasn't about dominance, it was about devotion. That real connection wasn't about how long I could last; it was about how deeply I could show up.

Let me make this clear, she loved my sex. She loved the way I handled her. The way I took control. The way I knew her body like it was mine. Her body was my playground.

But what made her different? She didn't just want me to perform; she wanted me to connect.

She would say, "You got the body part down. But I want you in it." Not just the man that could blow her back out—but the man that could meet her heart while doing it.

She told me how I made her comfortable expressing herself sexually. I unlocked her and opened her up to a whole new world. One that allowed her to open up sexually. I explored her body and gave her the freedom to let go.

She had always been in control in that area. Strong, disciplined, composed, always making sure everyone else was good.

But with me, she could unravel. She could lose track of time, space, and thought. She could go from poised to primal—because she trusted me with that side of her.

She told me I unlocked something in her. something wild, something free and not reckless—but real. Hearing that from a woman who doesn't open up easily. That hit differently.

We created a rhythm that was ours. One where she didn't have to lead. And I didn't have to question if I was enough.

There was no ego war, no pressure, just fire. mutual surrender. Two grown-ass people finally being met at their full capacity.

She didn't just slow me down. I turned her up.

And when I look back at those early moments, I realize we weren't just having sex. We were remembering parts of ourselves that we had forgotten even existed. The truth is, I never thought I was missing anything. I had been praised, respected, and bragged on. I had been a master at physical dominance. But emotional presence was a whole new lane.

She wasn't the type to fake it. She didn't exaggerate reactions to protect a man's ego. So, when she surrendered to me—fully, deeply—I knew it wasn't out of habit. It was out of trust.

It made me show up differently.

Every time she opened herself up more... every time I watched her let go of control and just feel... it wasn't just about sex anymore. It was spiritual without being religious. Sacred without needing ceremony.

We healed in those moments. Silently. Physically. Unapologetically.

I didn't need her to perform. She didn't need me to perform. We just needed each other to be real. And that's what changed the game.

Now I can say this with my chest: Yeah, I had great sex before. But with her, I found freedom.

And even better, I gave her the same.

**WACK 100 – EGO XPOSED TAKEAWAY:**

- I always knew how to handle a woman's body—but nobody ever taught me how to be present with her soul.

- R Ann B didn't need performance. She needed presence. That was a first for me.

- She loved my sex. She made sure I knew that. But she also wanted a connection. Eye contact. Vulnerability.

- She could feel when I drifted—even during intimacy. She'd stop me and say, "You left. Come back."

- That taught me sex wasn't just physical—it was emotional, mental, and energetic.

- I used to think slowing down meant being soft. I learned that slowing down is what creates depth.

- We didn't lose ourselves in each other. We found the parts we'd hidden from everyone else.

- I used to think great sex was about stamina. With her, I realized the real power was in connection.

- Making love to a woman who sees all of you— and still chooses to surrender? That's a different type of intimacy.

- She didn't just teach me how to make love— she made me want to.

# CHAPTER 7

# SHE LET ME LEAD BUT MADE ME EARN IT

# CHAPTER 7

# SHE LET ME LEAD—BUT MADE ME EARN IT

She wasn't impressed by titles. She was watching my tone. I thought leadership was automatic. That if I handled business, protected mine, and kept food on the table.

I thought any woman would naturally fall in line, especially since I've been carrying out these types of duties since I was 14 years old.

I had success and power. I had the presence that turned heads when I walked into a room. But she didn't flinch or move for titles. She moved for tone, peace, and leadership that made her feel safe, not silenced. And the truth is, R Ann B made me earn it. She didn't come with rebellion. She came with discernment.

She didn't push back to fight; instead, she paused to observe. She watched how I handled pressure. She paid attention to how I corrected her. Was I sharp, dismissive, or was I the man I claimed to be in public?

Behind closed doors, she tested my ability to lead with presence, not just power.

She was so smooth with it, I didn't even realize I was being tested—until I started failing the little moments I used to overlook. That's when I realized, you don't just receive a woman's submission, you earn it.

Not with control, with consistency. Not with money, with maturity. Not with force, with emotional intelligence. She didn't emasculate me; she didn't challenge my manhood. But she also didn't hand over her trust just because I showed up as "Wack 100.

She was watching Cash Jones. The man behind the interviews. Behind the headlines. Behind the empire. That's who had to lead her. Because you can't build a relationship off a stage name, you can't guide a grown ass woman with smoke and mirrors.

You must show up authentically, consistently and humbly. I couldn't just show up as a boss… I had to show up as a man.

Cash Jones was the businessman, father, and leader. And that's who she trusted, not saying I wasn't all of these things completely. There are parts of me I'd hold secret from R Ann B.

I wasn't out here trying to build anything new with just anybody. We just made sense; it was a perfect fit. The truth is, I hadn't really led in love before; to me, that's a weakness. It's about balance, too much of anything isn't good.

R Ann B didn't need a flashy man; she needed a faithful, consistent, consciously aware one. When she saw I was willing to grow into that, she started following in ways that made me feel like her king. Not because she submitted to pressure. I proved I could carry her purpose, not just her presence.

That's when I stopped moving like Wack and started showing up like Cash. The deeper she trusted me, the more intentional I became.

Not out of fear of losing her but out of respect for what she represented. She wasn't just a woman I was dating. She was a woman with vision, reach, and influence.

She trusted me to lead, so I had to show I could. That's not something you play with. That's something you protect, elevate, and cover. So, I started checking my tone, habits, and reactions.

She deserved a man who took her seriously. She wasn't just following my lead. She was following the fruit of my leadership. That changed everything.

**WACK 100 – EGO XPOSED TAKEAWAY:**

- Leadership isn't about who talks the loudest—it's about who moves with wisdom.

- She didn't need a man who controlled her. She needed one who could carry her.

- Emotional safety is what earns a woman's submission, not ego.

- I couldn't lead her as "Wack." I had to show up as Cash, the man behind the name.

- She didn't follow me because I was in charge. She followed me because I was accountable.

- She watched how I handled her purpose, not just her body.

- Real kings don't just want submission—they know how to steward it.

- Her trust refined me. Her standard elevated me.

- A woman like her doesn't follow blindly—she follows the man who consistently chooses growth.

So now? When people ask how I pulled a woman like R Ann B—

I tell them straight up:

"I didn't pull her; I grew into the kind of man she could trust and provoked her to become one with a reflection of herself."

That's the difference between being impressive... and being impactful. That's not Wack 100 talking. That's Cash Jones.

# CHAPTER 8

# SHE WASN'T MY ENDING

# SHE WAS MY BECOMING

# CHAPTER 8

# SHE WASN'T MY ENDING- SHE WAS MY BECOMING

"Every king has a crown, but not every man earns a kingdom." I've been known by a lot of names.

Wack, Boss, Executive, Shot Caller, and OG just to name a few. But the name that means the most now is her man. Because being her man required something none of those titles ever did, emotional accountability. Which requires presence, patience and peace. I used to lead from instinct and strategy.

Now I lead from intention; this wasn't about being in control. It was about learning to be consistent enough for a strong woman to rest in me.

Before her, I knew how to protect a woman. I've always known that. You come near what's mine the wrong way—and I'll shut it down, no hesitation. Protection isn't just about defense; it's also about direction.

She wasn't looking for a bodyguard. She was looking for a builder. A man with vision, a man with peace behind his power. A man who didn't just protect her body but could partner with her future.

That's where the shift happened. It wasn't about proving I could lead. It was about proving I could evolve and that our purpose could come into alignment. Not for her approval but for the man I knew I was meant to become.

A woman should connect with your future. She shouldn't just complement your life; she should challenge it. She should become a mirror that exposes your gaps and crowns your growth.

There was a time, she would say, I allowed other women to play in her face." Some of it might've been unintentional.

But the truth is, I didn't correct it. Not fast enough, not publicly enough. Not with the clarity a woman like her deserves.

What I didn't fully understand back then is that women have egos too. And the way you protect that ego as a man, especially when your woman is solid, loyal, and all-in, matters.

She didn't scream or throw things; she simply became a mirror. She started reflecting back the same energy I gave her.

That's when I realized, I didn't want to see her in pain. I could feel it. Her silence cut deeper than anything she could've said. And that's what broke me out of autopilot.

Because when you love a woman who holds you down at your worst, you don't play with her peace just because you're still learning how to move better.

She taught me how to treat her by showing me what it looked like when she stopped overcompensating for my mistakes.

That's when I adjusted.

Not just my actions but my awareness.

The deeper I fell for her, the more I understood:

Accountability isn't about being wrong; it's about being aware enough to grow.

I wasn't trying to hurt her. But I had to admit I was moving in ways that didn't protect her position.

When a woman feels unprotected emotionally, they don't just get quiet; they shift. Not because they stopped loving you, but because they started to love themselves enough to stop tolerating things that break their spirit.

Leadership isn't about how strong you talk.

It was about how responsible you are with her heart.

R Ann B never tried to check me in front of people. She never put my business on the internet. She carried it all like a real one.

But I saw her light dimming, not out of weakness. But because she didn't know how much longer she could protect a man who hadn't fully learned how to protect her heart, not just her body.

I couldn't take that, so I advanced to the next level.

Not because I was losing her, but because I finally realized what it meant to deserve her.

It wasn't about how many deals I closed, names I dropped, and money made. It's how I love her.

How I show up when no one's watching. How I respond when her soul is speaking, not just her mouth.

That's the part nobody teaches you as a man how to lead when the room is quiet, how to lead when she doesn't need a savior, but a partner in purpose.

That's where the real growth happened.

Not in the spotlight but in the silence.

It was the way I covered her name when she wasn't around. The way I protected her spirit, even when she wasn't saying a word.

The way I handled her vision was as if it were mine too.

Most women choosing to build with you are not asking for perfection. They are asking for alignment.

Now I'm aligned, clear and ready to build.

**WACK 100 – EGO XPOSED TAKEAWAY:**

- A woman doesn't just follow your power—she follows your peace.

- You can't claim a woman's loyalty if you don't protect her position.

- I didn't lose her—I evolved into the kind of man who could lead her right.

- She didn't need more of my dominance. She needed a version of me that could handle her destiny.

- Accountability isn't weakness—it's where real leadership begins.

- Emotional protection is just as important as physical presence.

- I didn't pull her—I provoked her to become one with the most elevated version of herself.

- My legacy isn't just what I leave behind. It's what I lead with.

- She wasn't my ending—she was my becoming.

# CHAPTER 9
## EGO ACLHEMY TURNING HEAT INTO GOLD

# CHAPTER 9

# EGO ALCHEMY — TURNING HEAT INTO GOLD

This ain't about just love anymore. It's about building an empire.

**R ANN B**

And building that empire almost cost me my voice.

There was a time when I sat back, watched him do his thing, and assisted. I waited in the background while he stood in the spotlight— And I watched as he screamed my name from every stage, every interview, every platform he touched.

I was grateful, but I wasn't expressing myself. I had no outlet. No space that felt like mine.

Before him, I was adored by both men and women. Not just because of how I looked… but because of my voice, my wisdom, my energy.

I had a club on Clubhouse called Love & R Ann B—
and it was thriving. When things got serious between
me and Wack, everything shifted. Some women pulled
back, and some stopped supporting me altogether.
Not because I changed, but because they wanted what
I had.

I also had to be careful with how I handled myself
because I wasn't single anymore. I didn't want to come
across as too friendly or flirtatious.

I started to feel like I had to shrink. Be careful how I
talk. Watch what I said. The same voice that once drew
admiration now made people feel threatened.

I let someone else run my club and slowly became
silent. Not because I didn't have something to say—
but because I didn't feel like there was space to say it.

## WACK 100

I didn't realize it right away. I was too busy yelling her
name loudly, thinking that was enough. I didn't see
that the same woman I was proud to have was starting
to dim the light that made her who she was before I
came.

When she finally told me how she felt, it hit me differently. Because all that time I thought I was showing her off—she was sitting in silence... wondering when her mic would turn back on.

**R ANN B**

And eventually, I got tired of waiting. I realized I didn't need permission to speak. I just needed space, so I made it. The funny part is he never silenced me, I was just so deeply in love. I became one with his vision, and all I wanted to do was serve him.

He didn't realize my support for him overshadowed how I showed up for myself. I didn't know that my showing up for him was showing up for myself because everything he did was not just for him. It was for US! I know I just said a lot, but read it slowly and you'll catch what I'm saying.

This book. This podcast. This movement—it's not just about us. It's about every woman who's ever made herself smaller in the name of love. For every man who never realized he was asking for silence instead of support.

**WACK 100**

Now, she got her mic back. I stand beside her—not in front of her. Because when two real ones stop trying to outshine each other, they light up the whole room.

**TOGETHER**

We didn't get here overnight.

It took a whole lot of unlearning, listening, and growing up in front of each other.

We're not just building love; we're building power with purpose.

And every scar, every silent moment, every ego check was part of the alchemy.

We don't have it all figured out, but we've figured out one thing that matters.

We're better when we build together. And that's what makes us dangerous in the best way.

## EGO XPOSED TAKEAWAYS:

- Two strong voices don't cancel each other out; they create harmony when aligned.

- Supporting someone loudly means nothing if they're suffering in silence.

- Power couples are not built on performance; they're built on partnership.

- When ego becomes a mirror instead of a mask, transformation begins.

- Shrinking for love is not love; it's suppression.

- Real love doesn't ask you to disappear; it invites you to expand.

- The most dangerous thing you can be is united and unapologetic.

# CHAPTER 10
# OUR RULES, OUR RHYTHM

# CHAPTER 10

# OUR RULES, OUR RHYTHM

Love without a plan is chaos with a good kiss. We knew early on that chemistry wasn't enough. Sex wasn't enough. Even growth wasn't enough.

What we needed was structure. Our own rhythm, rituals, and our own understanding of what we required to thrive. We're not trying to survive each other. We're trying to build with each other.

## R ANN B

We didn't follow anyone else's rulebook. There's no one-size-fits-all formula for two strong, experienced people coming together late in the game, with baggage, kids, careers, and real voices. So, we had to write our own rules.

Not because we're rebellious but because we're real. We had to ask each other: "What do you need in order to feel loved, respected, and safe?" And then… we had to actually honor it.

## WACK 100

It wasn't about being right. It was about being real. There were things I thought I knew about relationships, about being a man, about "leading"— but when I sat down with her, I realized leadership looks different when the woman in front of you ain't broken. She didn't need saving. She needed alignment, and once I understood that... I stopped leading from my past and started leading with presence.

## R ANN B

One of our key rules is to maintain a level of no ego during disagreements. That means no yelling to prove a point. No walking off mid-discussion. No, using "that's just how I am" as a shield to avoid growth. When you've both lived through enough chaos, peace becomes the real flex.

We made peace our baseline and rhythm our compass.

## WACK 100

We also had to figure out what worked for us, not what worked on the internet.

Sometimes that means I'm out handling business, and she's managing the home base, but don't get it twisted…

She's not "just" holding it down. She's running plays. She's building. She's making sure I'm not just moving but moving with purpose.

Other days, it's the reverse. She's in full motion; I fall back, supporting, protecting, and reinforcing. It's not 50/50, it's 100/100; whatever the day calls for.

## R ANN B

Our rhythm is sacred. We have rituals, daily check-ins, honest conversations, and sex that doesn't just feel good but brings us closer.

And when something feels off, we stop everything and get back in sync. There's nothing we're building that's worth more than the us we've built.

## WACK 100

That's what people don't see behind the scenes. It's not just love, it's not just business, it's not just sex, it's rhythm.

It's rules, the agreement that we ain't letting this slip.

This ain't a restart for us; it is the first time we're both doing it right.

## R ANN B

I used to feel like I had to choose:

Be the boss or be the soft woman. Be respected or be held. But now I realize... I can be all of it.

I can be powerful and poured into. I can build empires and still remain true to my femininity. I can run things, then curl up in his chest at the end of the day and let him lead with love.

That only became possible because we set our own rhythm. He didn't expect me to shrink. He just asked me to be real.

## WACK 100

And that honesty saved us more than once.

There were times we could've let miscommunication turn into disconnection.

Times we both had flashbacks of past relationships that made us react out of fear.

But we talked through it. Not after a week of silence, but that same day. Because letting things linger is how people who love each other end up strangers. Our rhythm is built on check-ins.

We ask each other:

- "Are you good?"
- "Do you feel heard?"
- "Are you holding back something to keep the peace?"

Those questions sound simple.

But they saved us.

**R ANN B**

Here's the truth: relationships don't die from a lack of love. They die from a lack of rhythm.

From going too long without syncing up. From performing instead of being present. From not paying attention when energy shifts. We don't do that anymore. Because we worked too hard for this. We have something we protect now—on purpose.

**WACK 100**

And everything we've built the bond, the brand, the movement—it all starts here.

Not in the spotlight, in the bedroom, on the mic. But in the quiet rhythm we return to when the world is too loud.

She's my peace, I'm her power and together, we're our own formula.

**TOGETHER:**

We don't follow trends.

We follow the truth, and the truth is that nobody can define us better than we can. We don't care how love looks on social media. We care how it feels when the doors are closed. We care about energy, effort, and intention. We don't chase perfection. We chase alignment. We've learned how to check in without ego. How to pause before reacting. How to lead each other without one of us feeling lost in the process. Our rhythm is ours. Our rules are written in honesty, not ego.

If you ever wonder how two bold, passionate, powerful people make love last? We make it ours. Every single day.

**EGO XPOSED TAKEAWAYS:**

- Love without structure turns into chaos disguised as passion.

- Rhythm isn't about routine; it's about alignment.

- Setting rules doesn't make a relationship rigid; it makes it intentional.

- Strong couples check in with each other, not just on each other.

- There's no such thing as 50/50—only what works for the two of you.

- You don't lose power by softening—you gain peace when it's with the right person.

- Real connection is built daily, not just in the highlight moments.

- When ego steps back, rhythm steps in.

# CHAPTER 11

# WHAT THEY DON'T SEE

# CHAPTER 11
## WHAT THEY DON'T SEE

They see the photos, hear the podcast, feel the chemistry, but they do not see the work, not the kind you post. The kind that humbles you. The kind that makes you sit in your ego and still choose softness.

The kind that doesn't come with likes, but comes with weight.

This love is layered, it's sharp and soft, strong and stretched. Everything we've built was earned in rooms nobody else had access to.

**R ANN B**

There were days when I felt like being quiet, and he made space for that. There were days I felt overwhelmed, and he didn't try to fix it; he just held me. He never asked me to stop being strong. But he did start reminding me it was okay to rest. Because what they don't see is how exhausting it is to be everybody's answer. To feel the weight your man carried because he, too, was everybody's answer.

## WACK 100

She manages numerous responsibilities. It took me a minute to realize that, just because she made it look so damn easy.

She didn't complain or break down in public. But behind the scenes, she's navigating pressure I never even knew how to name.

When I started really seeing her, not just loving her, everything shifted. I wanted to lighten her load; I wanted to see her get all her heart desired.

Now, I ask different questions. I check in before I check out. And I never assume silence means peace.

## R ANN B

He's loud in the world, but I know the quiet version of him. The one who replays conversations in his head when something didn't sit right. The one who feels everything but doesn't always know how to say it. The one who protects me with his whole chest, but sometimes forgets to protect himself emotionally.

What they don't see is that he's not just a provider. He's a man learning how to receive love, too. That takes strength most people never give men credit for.

**WACK 100**

People think I'm built for war. But she taught me how to be built for peace. I used to think love was about protection. Now I know it's about being present mentally and emotionally. Sometimes that means putting the phone down. Sometimes it means letting her lead.

Sometimes it means sitting in silence together without solving anything.

This love doesn't just talk back, it listens deep.

**R ANN B**

There's nothing glamorous about doing the work. But there's something holy about it. About showing up for each other when the world's too loud. About creating a language that only we speak. Falling back in sync after a disagreement without punishment or pride. We don't win because we're perfect. We win because we don't quit during the quiet seasons.

**WACK 100**

And when the world is watching, they'll never see the 3 AM check-in. The forehead kisses when words fall short. The small sacrifices we don't post but repeat daily. They won't see it, but we will always feel it.

**R ANN B**

We have boundaries that people will never understand. Not because we're controlling but because we're preserving what matters.

We don't entertain lies. We don't let outsiders speak on what they've never experienced. There are things we don't explain online. Things to which we won't respond. Because when you know what's sacred, you do not put it on the auction block.

What they don't see is the way we cover each other when we're not in the room. The way we guard the door to our love is like a vault because it is. What they don't see is the crashouts we have because I don't play when it comes to my man. How obsessed I am over him.

**WACK 100**

How I've had exercise on another level of discipline when it comes to her. I have changed in so many ways. Not just sexually but mentally and emotionally.

I had to unlearn habits that came from survival. I had to stop responding as if I were still in a war when I was finally safe. I had to close doors and set boundaries to doors I allowed to stay cracked.

She gave me peace. But I had to choose to stop fighting peace every time it showed up. A man can love you and still lose you if he lacks structure. So, I built some, not because she asked me to. She deserved all of me.

I refused to lose the one thing that finally made me feel seen. I love me some R Ann B.

## R ANN B

And I had to grow, too. I had to stop expecting him to read my mind. Stop weaponizing my silence when I felt hurt. Stop waiting for him to "just know" and start teaching him how to love me better with patience.

Because what they don't see is that I'm still learning too. I'm learning timing, when to address issues. How to shut up when he's frustrated and I have something to say. When he needs me soft and sensual, and when he needs me to be his slut. We're both students of each other. That's what makes this love different. We've learned how to teach one another on a daily basis.

## TOGETHER

What we have didn't come from luck. It came from work. Not just the loud kind, the silent kind.

The kind that happens in the middle of misunderstandings.

That shows up even when you're tired.

The kind that says, "We're not letting this fall apart over pride." People will see the surface and assume it's easy.

But what they don't see is what makes it sacred. We've cried, stretched, checked each other, and chosen this love on purpose.

We've rebuilt trust mid-conversation. We've chosen connection over ego, rhythm over routine, and truth over temporary validation.

So no, this isn't perfect; it's protected. And that's what makes it powerful.

**EGO XPOSED TAKEAWAYS:**

- The strongest relationships are held together by discipline, not display.
- Real love lives in the quiet work—the kind nobody claps for.
- Protecting your relationship sometimes means staying silent in public so you can be heard in private.

- Boundaries aren't walls; they're blueprints for protection.

- Love requires unlearning, relearning, and repeating until alignment is second nature.

- Leadership in love is about presence, not performance.

- When you're both students of each other, growth never stops.

- Sacred things don't need to be explained; they need to be guarded.

# CHAPTER 12
# EVERYTHING CAN'T COME
# WITH US

# CHAPTER 12
# EVERYTHING CAN'T COME WITH US

Growth feels good but what they don't tell you is… It is expensive.

We paid in silence, in distance, in letting go of people we once would've bled for. Not because we changed but because we evolved. Everything that was once tolerated no longer aligned.

## R ANN B

There came a point where I had to choose between protecting my peace and keeping access open for people who misused it. I had to unfollow energy that couldn't sit with my growth.

I had to unlearn the guilt I felt for outgrowing people who didn't want to grow with me. My mindset is that if the tree doesn't bear fruit, cut it off at the root and regroup. But Wack would say let it stay rooted a while to provide shade.

I'm a stern believer that when people show you who they are, move accordingly; you can't reward disloyal behavior. It hurts because I'm loyal, but loyalty without alignment is just spiritual self-sabotage.

**WACK 100**

You don't get to elevate and keep everything the same. It doesn't work like that. I used to try to make room for everybody, until I realized not everybody deserved the new version of me. That included friends and habits. Shit, it was time to cut anything that didn't serve where we were going.

**R ANN B**

The deeper our relationship became, the more I had to separate myself from distractions, not just people, but also patterns. I used to respond to everything. Now I protect my attention as if it were sacred. Especially being with a man like Wack. He came with built-in trolls who stayed in my DM, harassing me.

Not every DM needs a reply. Not every invite deserves a "yes." Not every crisis is my assignment. I don't owe my energy to confusion. So I kind of had a hard time understanding why Wack entertained so many confused people.

## WACK 100

It was easy for me to lend energy to what R Ann B would consider confusion, because to me it was a life-like video game. I enjoyed puppeteering and building my own characters. It kept me entertained and sharp. Truth is, I never cared about being outside. I've always been the type to stay close to my woman. I'm not the "boys' night out every weekend" type. That's never been me.

So when people say I "changed" because I don't pull up like I used to? Nah. I've always been like this. I just got louder about protecting my peace. I don't care about being polite. I care about being real.

If the energy's off, I'm gone. If I feel weird about how someone's moving around her or around us, I don't play fake. I speak on it. I move accordingly, and I never explain it. Because when you really have something to lose, you stop entertaining people who've got nothing to protect.

## R ANN B

As a couple, we had to start checking the room temperature, not just for each other, but around each other.

There were people close to us who smiled at our posts but secretly hoped we'd fold.

You could feel the tension. The competition.

The subtle shade. We didn't confront it. We just stopped allowing it near what was sacred.

## WACK 100

We don't do circles—we do alignment. You are either praying for us or plotting against us. Friends are potential enemies, and DNA makes you related; actions and deeds make you family. Ain't no in between. We don't hold grudges; we hold boundaries. And if the cost of keeping peace is distance, so be it.

## R ANN B

We had to check ourselves too.

Because it wasn't just people we had to leave behind, it was old mindsets. That "me first" mentality. That "I don't need nobody" energy.

That "I'm gonna do me, regardless" attitude.

That might work when you're single. But it kills the connection in a partnership. You can't build something real TOGETHER while still thinking like you're alone. We had to shift from "I" to "we," not just in words, but in how we move.

**WACK 100**

We no longer make selfish decisions.

We make US decisions. Because one wrong move from me affects her peace, and one misstep from her affects my purpose.

So, we talk differently now. We plan differently. We even rest differently. That old mindset of "I'm grown, I do what I want"? Yeah... Ok... that version of us doesn't live here anymore. That version doesn't make it where we're going.

## R ANN B

I had to learn that being in a relationship didn't mean losing myself. It did mean adjusting how I showed up. I used to move solo. If I wanted to leave town, I left. If I wanted to disappear and recharge, I did. But now, my peace isn't just mine, it's ours.

So I communicate differently. I move with us in mind. I don't just ask myself, "Is this good for me?" I ask, "Is this good for us? What would Wack think?" That's what love looks like when it matures.

## WACK 100

For me, it was learning how to slow down and actually invite her in. I was used to doing everything on my own. Used to solving, fixing, and handling. I wasn't used to asking for input or showing vulnerability.

When you're in a real partnership, you don't get points for carrying it all alone. So now I ask her opinion. I keep her in the loop. Not because I have to, but because her mind is sharp, and her heart is also tied to this vision. That was my adjustment. Realizing I didn't lose power by including her, I gained clarity.

## TOGETHER

We don't think like we used to. We don't move like we used to, and we damn sure don't love like we used to. Because elevation doesn't just change what's around you, it changes you. Everything that couldn't evolve with us?

Got left behind.

## EGO XPOSED TAKEAWAYS:

- Elevation isn't just about success; it's about elimination.

- Peace isn't found. It's enforced.

- Some people love the version of you that doesn't know how to say no.

- Loyalty without alignment is self-sabotage.

- Real love checks your mindset—not just your surroundings.

- You can't think like you're single and build like a couple.

- Protecting what's sacred means letting go of what's familiar.

93

- Discipline is more powerful than display—and more sustainable than popularity.
- Everything can't come with you—not even the old version of you.

# CHAPTER 13
# WE DON'T DISCONNECT

# CHAPTER 13
## WE DON'T DISCONNECT

It's easy to connect in the good times, but staying connected during pressure? That's the real work. This world is loud, our schedules are full, and life doesn't slow down just because you're in love.

That's why we decided early on:

We don't disconnect, emotionally, spiritually, or energetically.

Even when we're quiet. Even when we disagree.

Even when life is at its most challenging, we stay tethered.

**R ANN B**

There were moments I could feel him pulling away, not because of love, but because of the load.

Business was heavy. Family needed him. The world was calling for Wack 100…

But I still needed Cash.

So, I didn't wait in silence; I spoke up.

"Do you still feel me?" "Are we good?" "Do you still feel us?"

I learned to check the temperature before it boiled. What I realized is: silence can play tricks on your mind. When he gets quiet, my thoughts can get loud. Did I do something? Did I miss something? Is he distancing himself because of me or other factors?

That's why I'd rather risk over-communicating than sit in uncertainty. Because uncertainty will eat you alive faster than the truth ever could.

## WACK 100

She taught me that silence can become dangerous if it lingers too long. I used to think giving space was a sign of respect, but sometimes, she doesn't need space. She needs me.

Not a lecture. Not a fix. Just me.

I'd touch her hand, sit close, lock eyes with her and stare with a look of adoration. Sometimes presence resets the whole room better than words ever could. I would get a slight smile and a "why are you looking at me like that look. No words, all presence.

And I'll be real, sometimes men pull away not from pressure, but to dodge accountability. You don't want to face the argument. You don't want to hear her call you out. So you disappear into "quiet mode" and convince yourself you're keeping the peace. But really? You're just avoiding the conversation.

That's dangerous, because silence can feel like abandonment. When a woman who feels abandoned starts protecting herself, that's when love starts breaking down.

I had to learn that being present, even when I'm wrong, is better than pulling away. Because presence keeps the door open, silence slams it shut.

## R ANN B

Disconnection doesn't always announce itself. Sometimes it's subtle. Fewer laughs. Less eye contact. More distractions. You can be in the same house, the same bed and still feel like you're a world apart.

So I started checking in. Before we drifted too far to swim back, sometimes it wasn't about asking if we're okay. I wanted him to know I'm ready for the truth.

That's what accountability requires: a safe space to tell the truth without judgment.

If I want honesty, I must be a place where honesty can land. And to be honest, it doesn't always feel good.

**WACK 100**

We don't always speak the same love language, but we speak the same loyalty, even when I'm drained and being pulled ten different ways. Even when my mind is stuck on business. I still have to show up. This ain't the type of love you clock in and out of. This is the type you protect, even from drift.

You see, the thing about flexible women is they'll eventually start adjusting to the tone you set. So, it's best to check in emotionally.

And checking in doesn't always look romantic. Sometimes it's just a head nod in the middle of a crazy day. Sometimes it's her sliding in the passenger seat while I'm on a call, not saying a word, just being there. That's a connection too.

**R ANN B**

Some days I check in first, and some days he does. But we don't wait until things are broken to start caring. We check in while it's still working. That's why it works. And honestly, accountability is a love language too. Because what's the point of connection if we can't call each other higher?

Love without accountability is just comfort. But love with accountability, that's growth.

**WACK 100**

I've been in situations where I felt alone, carrying everything with nobody seeing me. This right here? This isn't that.

This connection knows when to lean in, when to fall back, and when to just sit still.

That's why I call her my avatar. When I'm overloaded, I plug into her. She doesn't drain me or pull at me. She aligns me. That's more than love. That's balance.

And I'll tell you sometimes that balance is just us on the couch, her feet on my lap while the TV's running. No words, no pressure, no performance. It's in those small moments that I remember why I don't disconnect. Because I'd rather share silence with her than conversation with anybody else, those are things you may never bounce back from.

### R ANN B

He's said that for a long time, but I didn't fully get it until I started watching the way he moves around me. When he's drained, my presence brings him back. Sometimes it's not about what I do. It's just about being there.

There's something sacred about how we recharge each other. He could be locked in on the TV, caught up in a documentary or a business call, but he still pulls me close.

At least half the week, we lay in bed together—naked, raw, real with the TV on, phone buzzing, and the world spinning. He makes room for me in the middle of it. He always reaches for me. Touches my back.

Pulls me into his space. We bond while the world does its thing in the background.

It's not always deep conversations. Sometimes we're just working, scrolling, laughing side by side. And somehow, that's when I feel closest to him. Because no matter what's on the screen, I'm still his favorite view.

Even when we disconnect for a little while, we never fully lose each other. He makes an effort to include me in everything. I know where his head is. I know what he's carrying. I don't have to guess.

That's what keeps us grounded. Even when we drift, we always find our way back.

**WACK 100**

At the end of the day, love doesn't mean much without consistency. I can't disappear just because I'm stressed. I can't shut down and leave her guessing. That's how people lose each other, slowly, silently.

So I made a choice: I stay plugged in.

Because when we're good, I move better in every area of life. She ain't just my peace. She's my reset, and I'd be a damn fool to disconnect from that.

## TOGETHER

We don't disconnect. Not for pride. Not for pressure. Not for performance. No matter what's going on out there, we choose to stay close.

## EGO XPOSED TAKEAWAYS:

- Disconnection doesn't always start loud; it starts subtly.

- You don't protect a connection by waiting until it breaks. You check in while it's still whole.

- Presence isn't about fixing, it's about feeling.

- The strongest couples don't perform connection; they prioritize it.

- Real love doesn't pull away when life gets loud; it leans in with intention.

- Being "busy" isn't an excuse when you love someone with clarity.

- Even in distraction, you can include each other.

- Skin-to-skin is sacred when it's built on trust, not performance.

- You don't always need a conversation. Sometimes you just need to be near.

- We don't always connect the same, but we never disconnect completely.

- She's not just his woman, she's his outlet, his avatar and is reset.

- Real love doesn't avoid drift. It learns how to swim back together.

- Avoiding accountability isn't peacekeeping; it's a form of disconnecting in disguise.

- Accountability is a love language. It's not about tearing each other down. It's about making sure you don't drift too far from who you promised to be.

# CHAPTER 14
# TRIGGERED BUT STILL CHOSEN

# CHAPTER 14

## TRIGGED BUT STILL CHOSEN

You can be healed and still get triggered. You can be in love and still feel fear. You can be deeply connected and still have moments where your past tries to take the mic. We learned that love isn't tested when everything's calm. It's tested when one of us gets hit with something old, unhealed, or unexpected.

But here's what we don't do: We don't weaponize each other's wounds. We don't run, we don't ghost, and we don't shame. Because when Ego wants to react, love chooses to stay.

### R ANN B

There were times he'd say something that didn't match my tone, and my body went straight into defense. Not because he was wrong, but because he brushed an old bruise. It wasn't him, but my trauma didn't care.

It whispered, "You're not safe." "You're not heard." "Leave before you get hurt." That's when I had to learn to pause, breathe and stop making him pay for echoes that didn't come from him.

Because the truth is, I'm not just in this relationship. I'm recovering from everything that came before it. But here's what mattered: he never made me feel crazy for being triggered.

**WACK 100**

When she gets quiet, I know she's thinking. When she gets still, I know she's sorting through her emotions. So instead of pressing her for answers, I give her space to feel.

I used to think triggered meant she was tripping. Now I know it just means her body's remembering something her mouth can't explain yet.

I don't take that as disrespect or let that push me away. I just sit with her through it. Because I'm not here to fix her. I'm here to be her safe place while she fixes it herself.

**R ANN B**

One of the most powerful moments in our relationship wasn't when I felt strong. It was when I felt triggered, and he still chose me.

He didn't withdraw, guilt-trip me, or make it about himself. He just said, "Take your time. I'm here when you're ready." That kind of love doesn't just calm your nerves; it rewrites the story.

**WACK 100**

I've been triggered, too. Sometimes I don't even realize it until I hear my tone. I'll snap without meaning to, get short or get cold. That's ego's defense mechanism, but she doesn't let me hide behind that.

She'll say, "Talk to me, not at me." "Where's that coming from?" And instead of arguing, I sit with it. I'd quickly realize she isn't trying to fight me, she's trying to reach me.

A lot of men use anger to cover up hurt. But all that does is push love further away. I had to learn that letting her in doesn't make me weak; it makes me accountable.

## R ANN B

We've both had to learn how to communicate through the storm. Not just defending our pain but understanding each other's pain.

Some days, that means talking it out. Some days, it's just holding hands until we come back down. But quitting? That's not an option.

## WACK 100

At the end of the day, it's about being present even when it's uncomfortable. Even when the old versions of us try to rise, even when it would be easier to shut down, we stay in it, we work through it, and choose each other every time.

## R ANN B

Let's be clear, being triggered doesn't always mean I'm unhealed. Sometimes it means I'm finally present enough to feel. You can be strong and still sensitive. You can be whole and still get activated.

Sometimes the trigger is just a signal that you're in new territory and that you're growing. What matters most isn't whether you get triggered; it's how you respond. I've learned to speak my truth without burning down the room. He's learned to stay with me through the fire. That's not damage, that's discipline. That's what makes love real.

## R ANN B

It's also important to communicate your triggers before they come up. Before you shut down. Before you explode. Wack and I have honest conversations about what triggers us. Not in an argument. Not in the heat of the moment. But in peace, when we can actually listen.

He told me what hurts him. I told him what drags me back to the old versions of myself. We talk about it and choose to unpack it. So, when it shows up later, it's not a surprise; it's a signal. That kind of communication builds trust. It builds awareness. It builds us.

**R ANN B**

And let's talk about how you respond when you trigger someone unknowingly matters. It's not enough to say, "That wasn't my intention."

You have to care about the impact. We've had those moments when one of us got hurt and the other didn't see it coming. But instead of getting defensive, we learned to get curious. What did I say, how did it land, and what did it bring up?

Because love isn't about never getting it wrong. It's about how you handle it when you do. Dismissing someone's feelings just because you didn't mean to hurt them is ego. That's not love.

**R ANN B**

Sometimes, triggering someone is like stepping on a landmine. You didn't know it was there. You didn't plant it. But now that you've stepped on it, you've got a choice. Lift your foot carelessly and blow everything up, apply the right pressure, stay calm, and listen to what they need to disarm it. That's what deep love looks like. It doesn't avoid the pain. It learns how to move through it without causing more damage.

**TOGETHER**

Triggers don't scare us anymore.

Because we realized that if we can survive ourselves, we can survive each other. No matter what rises, we rise together.

**EGO XPOSED TAKEAWAYS:**

- Being triggered doesn't mean you're unhealed; it means you're aware.

- Real love doesn't walk away when old wounds flare up.

- You don't fix your partner; you sit with them while they heal.

- Communicating your triggers before they show up builds safety.

- Defense is ego. Curiosity is love.

- Dismissing someone's feelings because you "didn't mean it" is still emotional harm.

- The way you respond when you trigger someone—especially unknowingly—shows your emotional maturity.

- Triggers don't have to become trauma when you treat them with care.

- Accountability doesn't require guilt; it requires presence.

- We don't avoid landmines. We learn how to step carefully through each other's past with grace.

- You can be triggered and still be chosen. You can be hurt and still be held.

- What matters most is: Do we rise together?

# CHAPTER 15
# SHE'S EMOTIONAL, HE'S DETACHED

# CHAPTER 15

# SHE'S EMOTIONAL, HE'S DETACHED

We used to think we were speaking different languages, me through feeling, him through silence. But the truth is, we were both saying the same thing: "See me. Hold me. Don't hurt me."

The world taught us that emotions divide men and women. But here's what we've learned: It's not emotion that creates conflict, it's ego.

The ego that tells him to shut down before he gets hurt. The ego that tells her to explode before she gets ignored. But love can't live where fear runs the room. This chapter is about unlearning the emotional habits we inherited and choosing presence over protection.

Because whether you cry loudly or shut down quietly, what you're really saying is: "I want to feel safe with you."

## WACK 100

See, most dudes ain't taught to feel, we're taught to fix. When she shares her feelings, I wonder what I'm supposed to do.

But it took me a minute to... she ain't always looking for a solution.

Sometimes she just wants to know I care. And that's hard for a man raised on survival, not softness. I didn't grow up in a household where emotions were openly discussed. You mad? Go fight.

You hurt? Man up. You crying? Now you the problem. So, when she brought me her pain, I was like... nah. I don't even know where to put that. But that's the problem—when a woman gives you her vulnerability and you reject it, you're not just hurting her. You're pushing her into silence. Silence is where resentment grows.

Have you ever been with someone who stopped talking just to protect themselves? It doesn't feel like peace; it feels like distance.

The real win in a relationship ain't being the calmest in the fight. It's being the one who says, Talk to me, even when your pride says Walk away. We're still learning, still unlearning. But now, when she says, "I feel like you're not hearing me," I don't just hear her, I listen to her.

## R ANN B

The world told me I was too emotional. Too reactive, too sensitive, and too much. Boy, was I misinformed: emotion isn't weakness, it's information. When a woman speaks from her emotions, it's not to manipulate, but to connect.

But how do you connect with someone who shuts down? Who zones out and acts like nothing is wrong? Here's what used to happen. I'd cry, he'd stare. I'd talk, he'd shut down, or it would turn into a screaming match.

I used to take his detachment personally, like I didn't matter. Like he didn't care, but what I learned is he wasn't ignoring me. He was avoiding himself. He didn't know how to hold my emotions—because no one ever taught him how to hold his. So eventually, I started withholding too.

Not just my words but my softness. I told myself, "If he doesn't care, I won't either."

But that's not power, that's protection, a defense mechanism. That's ego in a pink dress.

That's how two people end up sleeping next to each other, both starving for connection but too prideful to reach. I had to learn:

My emotions aren't a weapon, but they're also not a license to bleed all over him. There's a difference between expressing and exploding. I had to slow down… breathe… and invite him in.

Because sometimes, men don't fear emotion; they fear rejection. They fear failing in your eyes when they finally open up.

## PERSONAL MINDSET SHIFT

## WACK 100

There's a moment when you have to face your emotional poverty. You realize you know how to give money, attention, sex, and even protection.

But you don't know how to sit in her storm without trying to fix it. That's what love really is. Not solving her, but seeing her. Letting her feel without making her feel like a burden.

## R ANN B

It took me years to realize I wasn't "too much."

I was just too unfiltered for people who lacked the capacity to hold me. But in a relationship, your partner should be a safe place, not a shutdown.

And I had to ask myself: Am I loving someone who needs connection, or am I loving someone who needs control? Because ego will dress up detachment like discipline. When, really, it's fear wearing a fitted look.

## EXTRA PERSONAL LAYER

Inner Child Meets Adult Love

**R ANN B**

What I didn't realize at first was that sometimes, I wasn't arguing with the man in front of me. I was arguing with the little boy inside him. The one who was told: "Don't cry." "Don't feel." "Don't be soft." When I brought my emotions to him, I wasn't just asking for connection. I was unknowingly asking him to confront pain he tucked away decades ago.

**WACK 100**

Some of her reactions used to hit a nerve. Not because she was wrong, but because they brushed against wounds I never dealt with. It felt like she was questioning me, when really she was just trying to reach me. And for a man who's always been the protector, being emotionally present doesn't come with a blueprint.

It's not that I didn't care. It's that I was never taught how to be emotionally available without feeling like I was losing control. But love ain't about control. It's about staying in it, even when it feels uncomfortable. Not checking out or powering down. Just staying.

## EGO XPOSED TAKEAWAYS:

- Emotion is not the enemy; ego is.

- Women aren't "too much"; they're often too real for emotionally unavailable men.

- Detachment can look like peace, but it often hides fear.

- Men don't need to fix everything; sometimes, they just need to be present.

- Silence breeds resentment faster than arguments.

- Expressing emotion is not weakness; it's emotional fluency.

- Healing happens when we stop labelling and start listening.

- You can't love fully while emotionally avoiding.

- Feeling deeply isn't feminine, it's human.

- Connection begins when ego steps aside and presence takes the mic.

# CHAPTER 16

# CONTROL, SUBMISSION, & POWER

# CHAPTER 16
# CONTROL, SUBMISSION & POWER

Power in love is tricky, everybody wants it. But few know how to hold it without hurting the one they love. They thought leadership meant control.

I thought submission meant silence. We were both wrong. This chapter isn't about who's in charge. It's about how to lead without dominating. How to trust without disappearing. How to stop playing tug-of-war and start learning how to dance. Because real power doesn't need to prove anything, it protects, provides, and flows.

**WACK 100**

Let's get this out of the way: everybody wants power in a relationship. Even if you don't say it, you feel it. You want your voice to matter. You want respect when you speak. You want your word to mean something. That's power! But the problem starts when power turns into control. Or when submission gets confused with silence.

I used to think leadership meant making all of the decisions. The Final say and the loudest voice. But that doesn't make you a man; that just makes you loud.

Real leadership means taking responsibility. It means showing up when it's uncomfortable, when shit is messy. Showing up when she's emotional and you don't have the answers. If you can't create security, stability, and direction, why should she trust your lead?

A woman doesn't submit to control. She submits to confidence, clarity and consistency.

Some dudes want submission but haven't submitted to anything themselves. Not growth, accountability, discipline or even self-control. How do you want a woman to trust you when you don't even know where you're going?

It's not alpha energy if it's rooted in fear. It's not "head of household" if you disappear when pressure shows up. You can't earn submission by demanding it. You've got to live it and lead by example. Because when a woman decides whether she can lean in or needs to lean out, she's not just listening to your words, she's watching your actions.

That's what most men miss. You don't get to be the leader just because you're the biggest or the loudest. You lead by how you love, how you respond, and how you listen. If she trusts you with her submission, you'd better be worth the weight she's carrying behind you.

## R ANN B

People hear the word submission and immediately flinch. Especially women like me, who are strong, vocal, and driven. We've been conditioned to believe submission means losing yourself and silencing your voice. Becoming small so someone else can feel big. But let me be clear, submission is not weakness; it's not obedience. It's not giving up your power.

True submission is trusting someone enough to lean back, without falling. It's knowing that if I soften, he won't drop me. And here's the gag: most women don't mind submitting. What we mind is submitting to a man who hasn't proven he can lead.

There's a difference between masculine energy and manipulated control. Between leadership and dictatorship. Some men say they want a woman who listens. But what they really mean is, "I want a woman who won't challenge me."

That's not a partner, that's a puppet. And let's call it out, some women confuse control with protection. He checks your phone, isolates you, makes decisions for you, and you call it "love." Sis, that's not leadership. That's fear dressed up as dominance. It took me a long time to learn the difference. To see the red flags in a man who wants power but avoids responsibility.

See, submission isn't about losing your voice; it's about trusting who you allow to speak over it. When I say I'll submit, I don't mean I'll disappear. I mean, I'll support. I'll rest and I'll surrender control because I feel safe.

Baby, if I don't feel that, I will not be submitting.

If peace ain't present, I'm not falling back, I'm falling apart. So no, I'm not anti-submission, I'm anti-settling. I'm anti-following confusion. I refuse to submit to chaos dressed up as confidence. Because absolute submission doesn't feel like resistance, it feels like relief.

## PERSONAL MINDSET SHIFT

## R ANN B

For a long time, I thought being strong meant being in control. I associated softness with danger. Because every time I let my guard down, I get disappointed. So I started leading with power instead of peace. But that wasn't intimacy, that was fear dressed up as independence. What I realized is that I wasn't just protecting myself from him. I was protecting myself from my own vulnerability. And when a woman gets stuck in that space, submission doesn't feel like relief. It feels like a threat.

I had to ask myself: Am I holding the steering wheel because I want to? I'm scared he might crash us if I let go.

## WACK 100

I used to think that if I let her lead, I was less of a man. That if I didn't have the final say, I was slipping. But all that was ego in disguise. Truth is, when you're secure in who you are, you don't need to dominate everything.

What I've learned is this:

Leadership in love ain't about always being right. It's about being aligned. It's knowing when to drive and when to pull over and hear her GPS. It's knowing when to stand in front and protect and when to stand beside and support. The more I matured, the more I realized, she's not trying to control me. She's trying to connect with me when we both stopped fighting for power and started flowing in it.

### EGO XPOSED TAKEAWAYS:

- Power in love is not controlling; it's a responsibility.
- Submission isn't silent; it's trust, and trust must be earned.

- Control without clarity is just chaos in disguise.

- Women don't fear submission; they fear being led nowhere.

- You can't demand leadership if you avoid accountability.

- Real men lead through presence, not pressure.

- Real women submit through trust, not fear.

- Loud doesn't mean right. Quiet doesn't always mean safe.

- If peace isn't present, submission becomes a matter of survival.

- You're not fighting your partner; you're fighting your ego.

- When both people stop trying to win, love starts to flow.

- Control is ego. Alignment is power.

- Submission isn't gendered, it's relational.

- The strongest couples don't fight for control; they share the mission. You're not fighting your partner; you're fighting your ego.

- When both people stop trying to win, love starts to flow.

- Control is ego. Alignment is power.

- Submission isn't gendered, it's spiritual.

- The strongest couples don't fight for control; they share the mission.

# CHAPTER 17

# LOVE WITH CONDITIONS:

# THE HIDDEN CONTRACTS

# CHAPTER 17

## LOVE WITH CONDITIONS:

## THE HIDDEN CONTRACTS

We both had to realize that love doesn't come with a guarantee. However, it should also not come with a performance clause. If I have to shrink, tiptoe, or over-explain who I am to keep your love, that's not love—it's fear dressed up as commitment.

**WACK 100**

And if I'm holding her to expectations, I never even spoke out loud? That's not leadership, that's manipulation. Unspoken rules breed silent resentment. We had to start laying it all out: the fears, the triggers, and the truth. So we don't end up resenting each other for contracts we never signed.

This chapter isn't about blame. It's about awareness. Because if you don't speak your truth in love, you'll end up performing for someone who only knows the version of you that never rocked the boat. We're choosing to rock the boat together because that's the only way to learn how to sail through the storm.

## WACK 100

Everybody has terms. We just don't say 'em out loud. You walk into love thinking, "I ain't like your ex," but you still bring the same fears. Now you got two people in a relationship, playing roles to avoid rejection. And the second somebody breaks character, all hell breaks loose. Facts I ain't gon' lie. I used to keep a whole list in my head: She gotta act like this, talk like that, never do this, always do that.

But none of those rules were about her. They were about me needing to feel safe. They were about control disguised as standards. And the moment she didn't fit one? I'd check out emotionally like, "See? Knew this wouldn't work." That wasn't love. That was ego keeping receipts.

I used to think that if she changed, we'd be good. "If she stops nagging. If she's not so emotional..." But what I really meant was: "If she stops being herself, then I can handle her." That's the wild part. We say we want real love—but only if it fits our comfort zone. We ask for transparency, then punish people when it makes us uncomfortable.

And just like she said—those hidden clauses? Men see them too. Sometimes we ignore 'em because of ego. We see she's emotional, or quick to shut down, or carries triggers, but instead of respecting it, we think, "She'll adjust for me." We convince ourselves that love makes us the exception. Then later, we blame her for showing us who she already was.

The truth is, most of us are mad at people for not reading the fine print of a contract we never showed them. But sometimes, we're even mad they honored the fine print we ignored.

That's where ego sneaks in. Love becomes a courtroom. Now you're on trial for not being who I assumed you'd always be. But that ain't love, that's emotional blackmail. And if you can't love somebody when they're real. That ain't love either, that's ego with a leash.

Love only lasts if you let people grow, even when it stretches your comfort zone. Anything else is a cage.

## R ANN B

Here's what I had to unlearn:

Love doesn't require me to play a part. My power isn't lost when I lean in; it's revealed when I can surrender without sacrificing my identity. Real love doesn't ask me to be smaller. It asks me to be honest. It asks me to be safe enough to be soft. However, most people never reach that point, because they often lead with fear and mistakenly call it strength.

That's why so many women feel like they're failing in love, giving everything, yet it's never enough. It's not that they're failing. It's that they're performing under invisible contracts.

The fine print usually sounds like:

- I'll love you as long as you don't outgrow me.

- I'll stay as long as you never trigger me.

- I'll trust you as long as you're easy to handle.

And here's the part most of us don't want to admit: sometimes those hidden clauses are the red flags we choose to ignore. We saw the patterns. We felt the gut checks. We knew the terms were unfair. But we let love or lust blind us. We acted like we didn't read between the lines, even though the truth was right there in front of us.

Then, when it all fell apart, we blamed the other person. But the reality was—we ignored the contract, and pretended it didn't exist. That's not love. That's self-abandonment disguised as loyalty. I used to think being "ride or die" meant never leaving. Now I know it means being honest about what's not working even when it hurts.

Because conditional love says: "You're not the person I fell in love with." Unconditional love says: "I see how you're growing, and I'm growing with you." But that kind of love? It requires ego to sit all the way down. Conditional love always has a deadline. Performances end, and once the mask slips, the contract expires.

I had to face this: I wasn't exhausted from giving love. I was exhausted from negotiating my worth inside of it. I wasn't asking for too much. I was asking the wrong person to make space for all of me, not just the parts that were easy.

Real love doesn't say, "Be who I need you to be." It says, "Be yourself—and I'll meet you there."

**EGO XPOSED TAKEAWAYS:**

- Most people are in performance-based relationships without realizing it.

- Unspoken expectations are silent killers in love.

- Conditional love hides behind "standards" and "preferences."

- If your love has fine print, it's a contract, not a connection.

- You can't demand what you never communicated.

- Hidden clauses are often red flags we ignore, blinded by love or lust.

- Real love allows growth, not emotional blackmail.

- Don't ask for vulnerability and then punish it.

- If your presence requires performance, your love will expire.

- Performances end. Love endures.

# CHAPTER 18

# YOU CHEATED, BUT SO DID I

# CHAPTER 18

# YOU CHEATED, BUT SO DID I

There were moments we stayed, not because everything felt right. We stayed because we weren't ready to admit we were hurting each other in ways we didn't have the language for. It wasn't always physical. It was emotional. Silent contracts, unspoken terms. And when those got broken, so did we. This chapter isn't about blaming. It's about seeing. Seeing how ego can dress up as loyalty, how silence can feel like safety, and how performance can replace presence.

We had to learn how to stop hiding behind good intentions and start taking responsibility for the emotional weight we were both carrying because real love starts where ego ends.

**WACK 100**

Let me keep it real: there were moments when I gave energy I had no business giving. And it went further than just jokes and casual messages. There was a time

I entertained women in ways that crossed lines. Some of it was flirty. Some of it turned into sexting. Not physical but emotional. And yeah, it was betrayal. Because it gave someone else access to a part of me that was supposed to be hers.

I justified it like, "It's harmless." But the truth is, anything you have to hide has already crossed the line. I didn't sleep with anybody, but I played in a space that made her question her place. And if I'm being honest, I knew what I was doing. That attention fed something in me, something ego-driven.

I didn't want to talk about it because that would mean admitting I was wrong, and ego hates being exposed. So instead of being open, I got quiet, defensive, and tried to flip it on her like she was overreacting, but she wasn't. She felt the shift; she knew what was up. I disrespected the bond by making her question what was real. It wasn't just about what I said to them. It was about what I didn't say to her, what I didn't take responsibility for. That's the part that hurts the most— not what I did in the dark, but how I handled her when she brought it to light.

Let me keep it real—There were women I knew I had no business texting. I'd say it was innocent, but I knew better. I'd send the joke, knowing she'd laugh a little too hard. I'd drop the compliment, knowing it'd land a little too soft. And I'd justify it to myself like, "Woman, it's not that deep."

But here's the truth—

Any time I gave a piece of myself to someone who wasn't her, even if it was just attention, I was slowly breaking trust. Not just hers—mine too. Because I knew I was crossing lines, I'd be pissed if she crossed. I didn't want to have the conversation because talking about it meant taking accountability. It meant admitting I was still operating off ego, and ego doesn't like mirrors; it likes excuses. So I'd get quiet, dismissive and act like she was overreacting. Meanwhile, I was playing innocent while my loyalty was leaking. The way I pulled back without ever leaving.

And now I see it:

I didn't just cheat on her. I cheated us out of safety.

## R ANN B

I didn't cheat, but I did confide in the wrong people when I was betrayed. When I was hurting, I didn't take it to him. I didn't create space for us to work through the wound together. Instead, I took my pain outside the relationship and put it in the hands of people who weren't safe. Here's the danger in that: when you're vulnerable, you're open. When you're open, whoever you give your truth to has influence. Hurt and anger will have you saying things raw, unfiltered, and venomous. If the person listening is bitter themselves, they won't help you put the fire out; they'll add fuel to it.

Bitter men and women aren't safe places. They won't remind you to protect your home. They won't guide you back toward healing. They'll hand you validation when what you really need is direction. And validation feels good in the moment—but it keeps you circling the wound instead of treating it.

I thought I was "processing," but what I was really doing was leaking. Every vent, every late-night conversation, every unguarded confession was a piece of us I gave away. And that's the part I had to face, no, I didn't cheat—but I still betrayed our bond.

Because love is more than just who you sleep with. Love is who you confide in. Who you run to first when your world breaks. And every time I gave that to outsiders instead of him, I built walls between us that he didn't even know he had to climb.

That's how resentment sneaks in, not always from infidelity, but from misplacing intimacy. And intimacy doesn't always mean sex—it means access. And I had to admit: I gave too much access to the wrong people. I didn't take it to him.

Not because I didn't want to, but because he didn't want to talk. He didn't want to take accountability. When the person who hurt you refuses to hold you, you start looking for a place that feels safer. Sometimes that safety ain't physical. Sometimes, it's emotional. What made it worse was that I had actually permitted him. I said: If it ever gets to that point, just go through me, don't sneak. I tried to build something honest and open. But even with the door cracked, he still chose to climb out the window. And that left me confused. Was it the thrill of breaking the rules? Was it ego? Was it disrespect? Or was it just… disregard?

Because it's one thing to cheat, it's another to break the trust of someone who was willing to share power. I didn't feel insecure. I felt betrayed by someone I trusted to honor what we agreed on.

A woman's insecurity is not always her fault. Sometimes, a man creates it. Not by being abusive— but by being evasive. By not giving her peace in the area where she's already questioning herself. He'll say, "You're trippin." "That's not what I meant." "You're reading into it too much." When really, she's reading it just fine. She feels the shift. She hears what's not being said.

There were times he made me feel like I was imagining things. But he knew that attention from other women fed his ego. My doubt wasn't paranoia. It was my intuition screaming while he acted as if I were crazy. And that's the hardest part. Knowing your heart's not lying, but staying anyway, hoping your love will make him listen.

We're taught that insecurity is a flaw in women but praised as loyalty when it shows up in men. If she questions a woman's presence, she's "doing too much."

If he checks another man over her, it's "being a protector." But the truth is, insecurity and territorial energy are often the same emotion, just packaged with different gender privileges.

The real question is: What caused it? Because a woman isn't insecure for no reason. She's usually responding to the space her partner failed to secure. And when her concerns get dismissed, she doesn't feel reassured; she feels crazy. That's how love starts to rot quietly, not from cheating, but from the way we refuse to admit when we've made our person feel unsafe.

Ego won't let you say, "You're right." It'll say, "You're tripping." But love? Love says: "If something I'm doing is making you feel less than chosen, then let's deal with that—together."

## EGO XPOSED TAKEAWAYS:

- Cheating isn't always physical; emotional betrayal cuts just as deep.

- Confiding in the wrong person is often a symptom of feeling unheard at home.

- Silence in response to pain isn't peace—it's a lack of accountability.

- Emotional safety is built through presence, not just promises.

- Insecurity can be created by consistent emotional neglect.

- Double standards around jealousy and control need to be unlearned.

- Real love takes ownership—not just of actions, but of energy.

## TOGETHER

Infidelity isn't always physical. Sometimes, it's the slow erosion of emotional safety, the glances, the flirty texts, the missed conversations, the unspoken permissions betrayed. We both hurt each other in different ways, not through bodies, but through choices. One of us stepped outside. The other stayed silent in the pain. Both actions left wounds. What we learned is that betrayal is loud. Sometimes, it's in what you don't say, what you pretend not to notice. And what you allow to slide when your heart wants to scream. This chapter was never about pointing fingers. It's about tracing the pain back to where it started and deciding not to keep bleeding on each other.

Healing came when we stopped measuring betrayals and started unpacking why we didn't protect each other better in the first place.

# CHAPTER 19

## TRUST BEFORE LOVE

# CHAPTER 19
## TRUST BEFORE LOVE

From the start of this journey, we've shown you that ego can break a bond or build it. We've walked you through love, sex, power, and pain. But here's the truth we almost missed ourselves: none of it matters without trust. Love may spark the flame, but only trust keeps it burning.

### R ANN B

We were raised to chase love as if it were the prize. "If he loves you, you're safe. If she loves you, you're complete." But love without trust? That's just chaos in disguise. It looks like a connection, but it feels like confusion.

### WACK 100

Real talk—love is loud, but trust is quiet. Love is the "I got you." Trust is the proof behind it. I've seen women love men who earned nothing but their downfall. And I've seen men walk away from women who gave them everything—except safety.

## R ANN B

I used to give love as if it were owed. But I've learned love doesn't pay the rent if trust is missing. Because I can love a man and still not feel safe with him. And if I can't trust you with my truth, eventually, my love will freeze.

## WACK 100

I always say this:

"You can love your shoes, but can you trust them in the mud? You can love your hair, but can you trust it in the rain?" If the foundation is cracked, the whole structure is temporary.

I used to think being a man was about providing, protecting, and staying loyal to the house I built. But I didn't realize how shaky love feels when trust gets fractured.

## THE CONFESSION

Here's the kicker. I already had the green light. She gave me freedom, with boundaries. Respectful play, as long as it came through her. But I broke it. Not because I had to. Not because I didn't have options. But because I wanted to. Maybe it was the thrill. Maybe it was ego.

Maybe I didn't want accountability, even when I had permission. The act itself wasn't the real violation. It was secrecy, the disregard, the way I let her sit in silence while other women played in her face. Trust isn't something you get because you say "my bad." Trust is built in the moments when nobody's watching. When you shut it down, not because you're scared, but because you respect her.

And once I felt her silence, I knew—I wasn't just risking her love. I was risking her trust. That's the one thing you can't repair with flowers, apologies, or promises.

## THE TRUTH ABOUT WOMEN

## R ANN B

I loved him even when I didn't trust him. That's how women love, we give from emotion and then wonder why we don't feel safe.

He didn't have to sneak. He didn't have to lie. I gave him freedom with boundaries, and he still broke both. That's the betrayal. Women get labelled as insecure for calling it out. Men are called territorial, but women are called insecure. Nobody asks, "What did he do to make her feel secure in the first place?" That double standard doesn't just bruise us, it erases us. Until one day, we no longer recognize ourselves.

## THE LESSON

## WACK 100

I had to learn that trust doesn't live in your mouth; it lives in your patterns. You can't rebuild something you keep breaking. You can't ask for loyalty while living in the gray area.

# R ANN B

I used to measure love. Now I measure consistency. Because love can still confuse you, love can still hurt you. But trust? Trust is clarity. If I have to second-guess your words, your eyes, your loyalty, we don't have trust. We just have hope dressed up as love.

## EGO XPOSED TAKEAWAYS:

- Love without trust is gambling, you're betting on potential, not patterns.

- Respect is a man's love language. Safety is a woman's. Without both, love collapses.

- Honesty after the damage doesn't count. Prevention is what builds trust.

- Freedom in love isn't chaos—it's responsibility with room to breathe.

- Double standards kill intimacy. What's honorable for him should be honorable for her.

- Trust isn't just about cheating; it's about making someone feel safe, seen, and respected.

- Leadership is accountability—holding yourself before they have to.

- If love is the fire, trust is the wood. No foundation, no flame.

**WACK 100**

"I used to think being a man meant never needing permission. Now I know the real flex? Making her feel so respected, she gives it freely, not out of fear, but out of trust."

**R ANN B**

"They say love is a risk. But trust? Trust is the real investment. And if you can't protect what I gave you, don't ask me to rebuild it every time you burn it down."

**TOGETHER**

We thought this story was about love. We thought it was about trust. But what we've really been exposing is ego. Every fight, every breakdown, every lesson—it all comes back to ego.

The need to be right. The fear of being wrong. The pride that keeps us from admitting when we've already lost.

This chapter was the verdict: without trust, love doesn't last. But the final chapter? That's the execution. That's where we strip ego down to the bone and leave nothing to hide behind. Because if you thought this was raw... wait until you see ego, fully XPOSED.

# CHAPTER 20

# ALTERED EGO

# CHAPTER 20
## ALTERED EGO

We put our egos on to control what outsiders see, and often forget our partner can see right through that altered ego. We dress up our pain with power and call it confidence, but real connection starts when we strip all that off. When you can say, "This is me – unfiltered, unguarded, unfinished; – and your partner still stays, that's real.

**WACK 100**

I always knew who I was. The problem wasn't identity, it was expression. I had to learn how to show up without the extra armor. Not because I was soft, but because I was safe. With her, I didn't have to play a role. I could still be the man, still lead, still provide, but now I could feel too. That's not a weakness. That's grown-man clarity.

## R ANN B

He never needed to be saved; he just needed space to take off the mask. I didn't fall in love with the image. I fell in love with the man. But I had my own ego to strip, too. The one that said, don't be too soft. The one that said, stay strong and stay guarded. But the truth of the matter is, you can't bond through a bulletproof vest. Love requires skin, soul, and truth.

Sometimes, the ego isn't the enemy; it's a survival mechanism. It kept us protected in rooms where vulnerability was a liability. But in love? That same armor becomes a wall. We had to learn when to wear it and when to lay it down. You don't lose yourself by being vulnerable. You find out who's really there for you when the performance ends.

## EGO XPOSED TAKEAWAYS:

- Ego isn't always loud; sometimes it's silent, hiding behind over-achievement or emotional distance.

- We use altered egos to navigate the world, but forget to take them off in our most intimate spaces.

- Love reveals what the ego tries to protect: our fear of being unloved as we are.

- The right partner doesn't fall for the mask— they wait for the unveiling.

- Real leadership in love is learning how to lead without losing the softness underneath the armor.

## WACK 100

I never had a problem being strong. I had a problem being seen. Because when the world expects you to be solid 24/7, you start believing your own performance. But when she looked past the image and said, "I see you, but I miss you. Now that hit different. The ego is loud. But real love listens. And I had torn that presence ain't weakness, it's power in its purest form.

## R ANN B

I loved him before he knew how to lower his guard. But I didn't stay because of potential. I stayed because of progress. Because he wasn't just willing to show up. He was willing to shift. And that's what made me drop my own mask. We weren't perfect. We were present, and sometimes, that's the most powerful form of love.

# BONUS CHAPTER
# WHEN EGO ISN'T THE ENEMY

# BONUS CHAPTER
# WHEN EGO ISN'T THE ENEMY

It was never about destroying your ego. It was about making sure it wasn't driving the car.

Let's clear this up right now: The ego is not your enemy. It's your bodyguard. It jumps in when you feel exposed. It speaks up when you're about to be overlooked. It protects your heart like a Pitbull on a leash. But here's the catch: If you don't train it... It'll attack what's trying to love you.

Some of you were never the toxic one. You were just guarded. You loved hard, but with conditions. You gave, but only to those who never asked for your truth. You weren't broken, but you were exhausted. Sometimes, your ego stepped in because you were too tired to explain yourself again. We get it, but if you made it to this page? That means you're ready, not for perfection but for presence, partnership, and peace that doesn't require performance.

Because when the ego finally steps back, the real you gets to breathe. You've read our story. Felt our cracks. We witnessed our work. But now, the spotlight turns to you. What will you do with what you've unlearned? What kind of love are you prepared to receive now that you're no longer performing? Who do you need to forgive—including yourself- so that ego doesn't rob you of real connection again?

The ego served its purpose. It kept you safe. It built the walls. But now, it's time to build something better—together, not alone.

And that's the final truth: Ego isn't the villain. It just can't be the leader. Let your healed self lead this time.

## TOGETHER REFLECTION

### WACK 100

Real love doesn't need you to shrink. It just requires you to show up real. I ain't dropping my ego because I was weak. I dropped it because I wanted to win with her.

## R ANN B

And I didn't kill my ego. I just told it can't speak for me anymore. I'm still strong and bold. But now I lead with truth, not defense. And that's where the healing is. You don't have to erase your ego; you just have to stop letting it speak louder than your soul.

That little girl who learned to toughen up. That young boy who was told not to cry. They don't need more armor. They need freedom.

### EGO XPOSED TAKEAWAYS:

- Ego is not the enemy; it's the alarm system. Don't disconnect it. Just don't let it run the house.
- Real strength is vulnerability practiced in safe places.
- Love with armor is survival. Love without ego is healing.
- You can't heal if you're still trying to win.
- The most powerful thing you'll ever do is love without the need to control.

## POWERFUL CLOSING STATS

- 80% of couples say communication breakdown is the #1 reason their relationship ended—not cheating.

- Men are 3x more likely to shut down emotionally during conflict, while women are 2x more likely to overextend emotionally to fix it.

- Nearly 65% of women report feeling like they carry the emotional labor in their relationship.

- Couples who discuss emotional triggers openly are 70% more likely to report satisfaction in their relationship.

- The average couple waits six years of unhappiness before seeking help or making a major change.

- Ego, when left unchecked, is the silent killer of connection—but when exposed, it can become the bridge to deeper intimacy.

## R ANN B

If you've made it this far, I'd like to thank you personally not just for reading, but for being willing to confront yourself. This journey wasn't about tearing down; it was about truth. I hope you feel seen. I hope you feel challenged. And most of all, I hope you feel empowered to love harder, heal deeper, and stand stronger. Ego will always knock. Just don't let it answer for you.

## WACK 100

Real talk, I didn't think I'd ever be this open. But sometimes, the biggest flex is telling the truth about what you had to unlearn to grow. If this book gave you language for your silence, or helped you show up differently for the one you love—then we did what we came to do. Respect to everybody doing the work. Stay real!

# ABOUT THE AUTHORS

**R**Ann B (Rekeita A Bradford-Jones) is an author, motivational speaker, former ordained minister, and unapologetic voice for emotional truth and feminine power. Known for her raw delivery and fearless insight, she speaks directly to the heart of modern women navigating identity, relationships, and self-worth.

With a background rooted in ministry and a heart shaped by both trauma and triumph, R Ann B built herself from the ground up—becoming the emotional provider in rooms that rarely made space for her healing. Now, standing boldly in love, pleasure, and purpose, she writes not from the wounds but from the wisdom they left behind. As the co-host of the viral podcast **EGO XPOSED** alongside music executive Wack 100 (Cash Jones), R Ann B is redefining what it means to be both soft and strong, spiritual and sensual, healed and still evolving. Together, they bring unfiltered conversations about ego, power, gender roles, sex, and growth to the forefront of culture.

168

Whether on stage, on the mic, or on the page, Rekeita A Bradford-Jones is a force. And **EGO XPOSED** is just the beginning.

**Wack 100 (Cash Jones)** is a business owner, music and entertainment executive, and respected voice in the world of power, leadership, and loyalty. Known for his no-nonsense delivery and behind-the-scenes influence. He's negotiated multimillion-dollar deals, managed chart-topping artists, and built an empire that extends far beyond the mic.

But beyond the headlines and hustle is Cash Jones—a man who spent decades providing, protecting, and performing, often at the expense of emotional connection. **EGO XPOSED** is his most personal work to date. It's not about image or industry. It's about evolution. As the co-host of the viral **EGO XPOSED** podcast alongside R Ann B (Rekeita A Bradford-Jones), Wack 100 strips the mask and steps fully into presence, growth, and accountability.

He speaks for the men who were taught to lead with ego and shows what it looks like when a man decides to lead with emotional maturity instead.

From gang member to gatekeeper, from entertainer to executive, from provider to partner—Cash Jones isn't just telling his story. He's telling what's real.

# BIBLIOGRAPHY

**EGO XPOSED** is a raw, intimate work of nonfiction drawn from the lived experiences, relationship dynamics, emotional growth, and spiritual alignment of R Ann B (Rekeita A Bradford-Jones) and Wack 100 (Cash Jones). While every chapter is rooted in personal truth, the reflections are influenced by years of study, conversation, counselling, real-life ministry, and cultural observation—as well as the unspoken wisdom passed through pain, love, legacy, and ego death. The following texts, voices, and movements have either directly or indirectly informed the themes explored in this book.

## BOOKS &AMP; RELATIONSHIP THEORY

- Hooks, Bell. **All About Love: New Visions.** William Morrow, 2000.

- Perel, Esther. **Mating in Captivity: Unlocking Erotic Intelligence.** Harper, 2006.

- Brown, Brené. **Daring Greatly.** Avery, 2012.

- Thomas, Devon Franklin. **The Truth About Men: What Men and Women Need to Know.** Howard Books, 2019.

- Harvey, Steve. **Act Like a Lady, Think Like a Man**. Amistad, 2009.

- Davis, Angela Y. **Women, Race, & Class**. Vintage, 1983.

- Tolle, Eckhart. **The Power of Now**. New World Library, 1997.

- Gray, John. **Men Are from Mars; Women Are from Venus.** HarperCollins, 1992.

- Glover, Robert. **No More Mr. Nice Guy**. Running Press, 2003.

- Deida, David. **The Way of the Superior Man**. Sounds True, 2004. Spiritual Influence

- The Bible, King James Version – Referenced in relation to spiritual order, submission, accountability, and the sacred role of a woman's first ministry being her household.

- Proverbs 31 and Ephesians 5 – Foundational scriptures echoed throughout the themes of leadership, love, and mutual respect.

- Therapeutic & Emotional Intelligence Sources

- Gottman, John and Julie. **Eight Dates: Essential Conversations for a Lifetime of Love**. Workman Publishing, 2019.

- Levine, Amir and Heller, Rachel. **Attached: The New Science of Adult Attachment.** Tarcher Perigee, 2010.

- Winch, Guy. **Emotional First Aid**. Plume, 2014.

- Townsend, Dr. John. **Boundaries in Marriage**. Zondervan, 1999.

## CULTURAL &AMP; HIP-HOP INFLUENCE

- Tupac Shakur – Lyrics, interviews, and poetic vulnerability that shaped a generation's view of masculinity, pain, and duality.

- Jay-Z, **4:44** – A sonic exploration of infidelity, ego death, and Black legacy that mirrored many themes in this book.

- Lauryn Hill, **The Miseducation of Lauryn Hill** – A feminine blueprint for truth-telling, heartbreak, and soul recovery.
- Nipsey Hussle – His message of legacy, loyalty, and partnership echoes through the dynamic between power couples who build together.

## OTHER SOURCES OF INSPIRATION

- "EGO XPOSED" Podcast (2025), hosted by R Ann B and Wack 100 — A documented archive of vulnerability, transparency, growth, and unfiltered relationship evolution.
- Instagram, Clubhouse, YouTube, and TikTok commentary (2022–2025) — Real-time relationship debates and community conversations that inspired chapter content and reflections.
- Private therapy sessions, coaching, and lived ministry experience by R Ann B.
- Real conversations, heartbreak, recovery, and love between Cash Jones (Wack 100) and R Ann B, 2022–2025.

www.ingramcontent.com/pod-product-compliance
Lightning Source LLC
Chambersburg PA
CBHW070040100426
42740CB00013B/2736